"*The Turbulent Twenties Survival Guide* is truly a remarkable and much needed guide to life after college. It will help young people deal with the psychological challenges that arise upon graduation from college. A must read!"

> —*Ronald F. Levant, Ed.D., ABPP, dean and*
> *professor of psychology at the University of Akron*
> *and coeditor of* A New Psychology of Men

"In *The Turbulent Twenties Survival Guide,* Salazar asks the questions about 'real life' that are on the minds of most recent college graduates. And he provides answers, based on cutting-edge psychological research, that are thoughtful, cogent, practical, and accessible. This is a fine book."

> —*Barry Schwartz, Ph.D., Dorwin Cartwright*
> *Professor of Social Theory and Social Action at*
> *Swarthmore College and author of* The Paradox
> of Choice: Why More Is Less.

"A useful and informative guide to the challenges faced by today's emerging adults in work, in their personal lives, and in developing their own identities. It is refreshing that Salazar does not simply regard the twenties as a "crisis" period but shows the importance of seeing it as a decade full of promising possibilities. This book will help emerging adults to make the most of their twenties."

> —*Jeffrey Jensen Arnett, Ph.D., research professor at*
> *Clark University and author of* Emerging
> Adulthood: The Winding Road from the
> Late Teens Through the Twenties

"Salazar brilliantly reaches out to a segment of the population that is typically overlooked by self-help books. Although there are many books addressing the concerns of toddlers, adolescents, middle-aged people, and senior citizens, scant attention has been given to the trials and tribulations of young adults. *The Turbulent Twenties Survival Guide* spells out the challenges encountered by young people as they venture from the security of the academic world into the turbulence of post-college life. In Salazar's book young adults are provided with provocative questions to contemplate as well as specific strategies to tap as they respond to life in the real world. Twentysomething readers will be relieved and grateful to realize that the difficulties they face are also being encountered by a countless number of their peers. Such a realization will lighten their emotional burden so that they can solve the problems of this stage of life while they continue to grow and to prepare themselves for the next developmental tasks that await them."

—Richard P. Halgin, Ph.D., professor of psychology
at the University of Massachusetts at Amherst

turbulent twenties
survival guide

figuring out
who you are,
what you want &
where you're going
after college

marcos r. salazar

New Harbinger Publications, Inc.

Publisher's Note

Distributed in Canada by Raincoast Books.

Copyright © 2006 by Marcos Salazar
New Harbinger Publications, Inc.
5674 Shattuck Avenue
Oakland, CA 94609
www.newharbinger.com

Cover design by Amy Shoup; Text design by Amy Shoup and Michele Waters-Kermes; Acquired by Tesilya Hanauer

All Rights Reserved. Printed in the United States of America.

Library of Congress Cataloging-in-Publication Data

Salazar, Marcos.
   The turbulent twenties survival guide : figuring out who you are, what you want, and where you're going after college / Marcos Salazar.
       p. cm.
    ISBN 1-57224-421-6
    1. Young adults—Life skills guides. 2. College graduates—Life skills guides. 3. Young adults—Psychology. I. Title.

   HQ799.5.S19 2006
   646.70084'2—dc22

                          2005037932

08 07 06

10 9 8 7 6 5 4 3 2 1

First printing

contents

acknowledgments

This book wouldn't have been possible without the thousands of conversations over the years with all the fellow twentysomethings I've encountered since my own graduation. I thank you for opening yourselves up and telling me your pains, frustrations, and defeats, as well as your joys and triumphs. I'd like to say thanks to Mike Collins and Ryland Witten-Smith for listening to my own challenges with the turbulent twenties, as well as talking through some early ideas for the book. I'd like to thank my former agent, Kimberly Valentini, for taking a chance on a manuscript in rough form. I want to express my appreciation to Tesilya Hanauer at New Harbinger Publications for all the editorial guidance through the publication process. You and Heather Mitchener helped make the manuscript become what I envisioned it to be many years ago, and I am eternally grateful. Thanks to Carole Honeychurch for such greats edits in tightening up the book. I have become a better writer because of your suggestions. And lastly, I'd like to thank my parents, Orlando and Sarah Salazar, for all the love they have given me since graduating college. You have supported me in all the paths I have explored in trying to figure out who I am and who I want to become, and I can't think of anything better for a parent to do for their twentysomething child.

introduction

It wasn't too hard to see the frustration on her face when she told us, "There really isn't a guide on how to live your life after college!" A group of friends and I were having some drinks on a nice summer day when Heather, a twenty-six-year-old friend of a friend, happened to join us. When she walked up to our table, I noticed that her demeanor didn't fit too well with the beautiful weather that sunny day. You could clearly see that something heavy was weighing on her mind, and it looked like it had been there for quite some time. She grabbed a seat across from me and as we chatted about our lives and what had brought us to Washington, DC, I happened to mention that I was working on a book about the psychology of life after college. As I began telling her that the book was about the new challenges twentysomethings were facing as they made the transition from college to today's working world, I could see I'd piqued her interest. What I soon realized was that by mentioning the topic of the book, I had turned on an emotional faucet within her. In an instant she quickly started pouring out all the personal struggles she had grappled with since leaving college.

She began to talk about how lost she'd felt since graduation and how she didn't really know what she wanted to do with her life. She spoke about hating her job and wanting to quit so she could move somewhere new. But almost in the same breath she mentioned that she wasn't sure what she would do if she moved because she didn't have much money and it was hard to find a good job with just a college degree. Her words sounded really familiar to me. I could easily empathize because, not only did I go through my own personal struggles after graduation, but I also had heard this kind of experience time and time again from almost every twentysomething I had encountered.

It was after her catharsis about postcollege life that Heather complained that she couldn't even find much guidance about how to get through this period. "I mean," she laughed, "why can't there be some sort of guidebook for this stuff?" This didn't surprise me because other twentysomethings had told me the exact same thing and each time I heard them say it, I knew they weren't talking about a guide on how to write a resumé, find an apartment, or explain a 401(k). Yes, these were important aspects of postcollege life, but what twentysomethings were really looking for was a book that helps graduates deal with all the psychological challenges that arise the moment they leave college and begin the rest of their lives. This need is the reason I decided to write *The Turbulent Twenties Survival Guide.*

graduation and the loss of identity

When graduation came around, I really didn't know exactly what I wanted to do with my life, so I moved around quite a bit. First, I moved to New Haven, then to Boston, Washington, DC, Taos, New Mexico, Barcelona, again to Taos, and finally back to DC—all in the span of a few years. Not only did I hop around from city to city, but I also hopped from job to job. First I was a personal trainer, then an intern for a political nonprofit, a cycling instructor, a substitute teacher, a case manager at a mental health clinic, a born-again student in Barcelona, a gym membership salesman, and finally, a researcher at the American Psychological Association. I was all over the place my first years out, and what I quickly learned during my postcollege journey was that I wasn't alone.

During my travels I encountered a wide array of twentysomethings who were doing the exact same thing I was. And it wasn't a specific type of twentysomething either. I met recent graduates at various points during their twenties who went to many different sizes and types of schools, majored in everything from Spanish to neuroscience, and came from every socioeconomic background. As a psychologist by nature, I would always ask them about their travels, and what I found was that people in their twenties were constantly hopping from job to job and city to city in search of what seemed to be something that their current lives were not providing them. As I continued to listen to all their stories, I realized that there was something we all had in common that was at the heart of today's postcollege experience: after graduation, all the rules of life completely change. The educational structure we've lived in since childhood completely disintegrates, and we are forced to shed the identity of a student. What we then do during our twenties is search for a new identity to help steer us through the world we'll be living in for the rest of our lives.

a search for a new vision of self

Growing up, life mostly revolved around being a student inside a highly structured educational system. There was always a detailed path laid out for you with clear, specific goals to achieve at every level of the system. Academic rites of passage such as papers, exams, and the SATs gave your life purpose and direction all the way up until college graduation. In this familiar academic world, you always knew what to expect and how to apply your intellectual skills to accomplish all that you needed to. And if you had questions, there were resources available to help. But this all changes as soon as you grab your diploma and say good-bye to the college campus.

After graduation, the educational path you've followed all your life disappears and you're forced to create your own structure and a revised identity in a whole new world outside of school. This major life transition quickly triggers an intense period of reevaluating *who you are* and *who you want to become*—two psychological processes I describe as a search for a new *vision of self*. This search is a universal experience among graduates, and it all stems from having to answer that one basic question that confronts you as soon as you accept your diploma: What do I want to do with the rest of my life? However, as soon as you ask this existential question, you quickly realize that there isn't a clear and easy answer. In fact, by asking it you open up the floodgates to countless others: Who am I? Who do I want to become? Where am I going? What are my passions in life? Which direction do I want to go in? How do I deal with all the choices out there? Am I making the right decisions? Why is the real world so different than I pictured it? Why is it so difficult to meet people? Will I achieve all the dreams I had in college? Will I ever find a job that I love? Am I an adult? Will I ever truly be happy?

These are some of the thoughts that can plague your consciousness after graduation. These are the soul-searching questions that can keep you awake until three in the morning, and no matter how much you try to ignore or delay answering them, they are always there in the back of your mind, waiting for you to respond. They pop up the moment you leave college, on the first day of your job, when you try to meet new friends, when you go out on a first date, when you wake up in the morning to go to work, and each night when you go to bed. The search for answers to these questions is one of the most important challenges—as well as one of the greatest opportunities— that you'll experience during your postcollege years, and the methods you use in answering them will eventually determine the kind of life you create for yourself during your twenties.

new-world rules, old-school tools

But let's be honest here: we're not the first generation to travel through school and make the transition into the working world. Millions of college graduates in the past have done it, so what makes today's twentysomethings so special that they need a guide to life in the twenty-first century? Why not use the advice given to previous generations: "Study hard, get good grades, go to college, find a steady job, get married, buy a house, raise a couple of kids, and have a nice life." It certainly wasn't a smooth ride for everyone, but this life philosophy provided a solid line to follow and was a logical path for success and stability. So, the obvious truth is that leaving academia and entering the working world is not unique to our generation. However, the world today's twentysomethings are entering into after graduation is not the same one their parents transitioned into during their twenties. What emerged at the end of the twentieth century was a new social and economic reality, making the advice used by previous generations inapplicable to many of the challenges that twentysomethings face today.

We live in a global economy characterized by accelerated scientific and technological breakthroughs, rapid change, endless amounts of information, and an unprecedented level of choice. When I graduated college in 2000, we were at a peak of this information-age economy with the dot-com boom. The kind of workers that were in demand then were people who were good at applying theoretical and analytical knowledge, such as computer programmers who could crank out code or MBAs who could crunch numbers. But just a few years later, this is no longer the case. As psychologist Daniel Goleman, author of the best-selling book *Working with Emotional Intelligence*, has found during his research:

> The rules for work are changing. We are being judged by a new yardstick: not just by how smart we are or by our training and expertise, but also by how we handle ourselves and others ... these rules have little to do with what we are told

is important in school; academic abilities are largely irrelevant to this standard. The new measure takes for granted having enough intellectual ability and technical know-how to do our jobs; it focuses instead on personal qualities, such as initiative and empathy, adaptability and persuasiveness (1998, 3).

In the past, young people were told that math, science, and technical skills were a permanent ticket to success, and much of today's educational system is still a reflection of this thinking. However, more and more psychological research is showing that success in today's new economy takes much more than intellectual excellence, technical expertise, and "book smarts." What is required is a new kind of intelligence—psychological intelligence—and this shift can be seen in what businesses are wanting in new hires. In a national survey by Anthony Carnevale and his colleagues, employers were asked what they were looking for in entry-level workers (1990). Out of seven desired traits that were listed, only *one* was academic: competence in reading, writing, and math. All the others were psychological in nature, and what Goleman and other psychologists have found is that in order to succeed in today's working world, a different type of intelligence is needed that includes psychological skills such as:

- high levels of self-awareness

- strong self-esteem

- regulation of one's emotional state

- initiative and self-motivation

- discipline and persistence

- empathy and relationship building

- conflict management

- optimism

- decision-making skills

- goal setting and big-picture thinking

- innovation and entrepreneurship

- creativity

- leadership

But if you look at the skills above, how many of them were directly taught to you during your educational career? Probably none of them, and a major problem that today's graduates are facing is that they're coming out of college equipped with a set of skills that are becoming less and less important in today's working world. As Goleman explains, "… your ability to perform at peak depends to a very great extent on your having these abilities—though almost certainly you were never taught them in school. Even so, your career will depend, to a greater or lesser extent, on how well you have mastered these capacities" (1998, 4).

Now, my point here is not to bash our educational system. I loved my college experience and wouldn't trade it for anything in the world. However, we must acknowledge and accept that the rules of the working world are rapidly transforming, and as they continue to change and evolve, so do the skills that graduates need. Since our educational system is not providing twentysomethings with these skills, one of the main purposes of *The Turbulent Twenties Survival Guide* is to show how you can develop the kind of psychological intelligence that is becoming indispensable in today's ever-changing, ultra-competitive global economy.

the ever-changing generation

There has never been a generation that has grown up in a time of such extraordinary wealth than ours. The information age has provided us an unprecedented level of freedom, an unlimited amount of choice, and more material comforts than ever before. We have grown up with cell phones, BlackBerries, and iPods and are super savvy with all the technological gadgets that come out almost on a daily basis. We've lived in a time when computers and the Internet affect virtually every aspect of our personal and professional lives, and anything we want to know is just a Google search away. As psychologist Jane Brown from the University of North Carolina at Chapel Hill explains in *Emerging Adults in America: Coming of Age in the Twenty-first Century*:

> They are the first to have grown up learning their ABCs on a keyboard in front of a computer screen, playing games in virtual environments rather than backyards or neighborhood streets, making friends with people they have never and may never meet through internet chat rooms, and creating custom CDs for themselves and their friends. This new media environment is dramatically different from the one in which their parents grew up because it is more accessible, more interactive, and more under their control than any ever known before (2005, 279).

We are also the most mobile and traveled generation in history. Many of us moved away for college, studied abroad for a semester or two, and now, during our twenties, constantly move from job to job and venture off to new cities every couple of years. We are in no hurry to achieve traditional markers of adulthood such as picking a set career, getting married and raising a family, or buying our first home. We simply want to experience all that life has to offer and don't mind taking our time to do so.

Now, do these many "firsts" combined with the new psychological challenges that twentysomethings are facing after college mean that a new generation is emerging? Recently, there's been an attempt to stamp a number of different labels on today's twentysomethings. Names like "adulescents," "thresholders," "kiddles," and "twixters" have all been used to try to describe our generation. But the truth is, these labels sound more like names for candy bars and dog food rather than terms describing what our generation is experiencing at the beginning of the twenty-first century. As a twentysomething, when I hear these names I not only cringe, but feel insulted, because these labels have a negative connotation and, quite frankly, are condescending. None of these terms address the myriad of issues twentysomethings are dealing with today. The truth is we are an *ever-changing generation*, constantly transforming ourselves and our lives just as rapidly as the constantly changing world around us. This is why lumping twentysomethings into fleeting categories will never work. Instead of trying to put a whole generation of young people into a box with trendy names, it is much more constructive to provide a description that encapsulates the ever-changing lives of this generation. More importantly, it is essential to understand what actually has been created: a new and distinct transitional period after college called the turbulent twenties.

a crisis or grand opportunity?

Over the past few years there's been talk about how today's postcollege transition will cause you to experience a "crisis" during your twenties. Joining the ever-popular adolescent crisis, thirtysomething crisis, and mid-life crisis, if we were to follow this rationale by adding a quarter-life crisis to the list, it would mean our entire life is just one big crisis! Now, it's true that twentysomethings who are unable or refuse to deal with the challenges of the turbulent twenties can develop serious psychological problems, such as intense feelings of doubt, anxiety, and depression—what I describe as the *postcollege blues*. But to label this whole period in life as a crisis is to subscribe to the view that life is something that one must endure rather than explore and enjoy. To believe that life during your twenties is eventually going to turn into a crisis is to expect to be automatically doomed after graduation. Instead, I will try to take a much more optimistic approach to what graduates are experiencing after college because our twenties don't have to be all about stress, frustration, and disappointment. Rather, this time can be a great opportunity for self-discovery, self-fulfillment, and self-actualization.

a different book for your twenties

Now, I want to point out that this book is not one of those resumé-building, cover-letter-writing, apartment-finding, after-college books that you can find on store shelves today. Yes, these are important aspects of twentysomething life. However, what books like those have ignored is the major psychological component to these postcollege issues. What makes *The Turbulent Twenties Survival Guide* so different is that it's the first book to help twentysomethings develop the psychological insight needed to adequately cope with the new and unique challenges you will face in all aspects of your postcollege life. What I've discovered during my research is that it's extremely difficult, if not impossible, to effectively do all the things that those other books talk about if you're struggling psychologically and unable to cope with the challenges and daily stress of the turbulent twenties. This book seeks to remedy this problem by combining clinically tested psychological strategies with real-world advice from twentysomethings to provide you with everything you need for dealing with all the challenges you face during your postcollege years.

I also want to emphasize that just because the knowledge in this book will help you cope, it won't stop you from having the challenges you face after college. While developing the psychological intelligence needed to adapt to the turbulent twenties is a vital component to becoming mentally healthy during this period in life, it's not the sole element involved in your emotional well-being. You may still be prone to the postcollege blues when faced with the challenges and hazards of the turbulent twenties. However, those twentysomethings who face the realities of postcollege life and make a conscious effort to seek out the knowledge and develop the skills outlined in this book will be much more resilient. When you take this book to heart, you'll be better equipped to cope with life's adversities and less likely to surrender to hopelessness and defeat.

your after-college road map

While writing this book I've been fortunate enough to work at the American Psychological Association, gaining access to the most cutting-edge psychological research available today. However, there is a problem with lots of this life-changing research—it's mostly written for professionals or academics. Most everyday people don't have the time to wade through the jargon and academic language to get to the truth beneath. What I've done in *The Turbulent Twenties Survival Guide* is translate this knowledge so you can use it in real life. I've taken the latest psychological research and applied it to what our generation is going through to not only explain the causes of the turbulent twenties but also to show you how to increase your psychological intelligence to create all the solutions you'll need.

In chapter 1, I will discuss the psychology of the identity shift that takes place as you make the transition from college to the working world. I begin with this aspect of your vision of self because before you can move forward in figuring out who you want to become and what type of life you want to create for yourself, it is vital to develop a solid sense of who you are. In chapters 2 and 3, we'll look at the factors that influence who you want to become and examine the psychological skills needed to adapt and thrive in today's turbulent twenties. In chapter 4, we'll explore how to conquer the postcollege blues by using clinical psychology techniques to make sure that you are mentally strong during your twenties. Then in chapters 5 and 6, I will show you how to apply your psychological intelligence skills to your professional and social life.

It is essential that you read the book from beginning to end, because each chapter builds upon the preceding one. Reading straight through will ensure that you get the most out of this guide. At the end of each chapter you will also find a list of the best psychological books related to each of the topics I discuss. I highly recommend reading these valuable resources. They are written by some of the most amazing psychologists and writers today and will help you to further develop the psychological skills needed to make the hopes and dreams you had in college a reality today.

developing your psychological intelligence

Throughout this book you will find questions to answer and psychological exercises to complete. While you may say to yourself, "Who really does these self-help exercises?" a great deal of psychological research shows that people who engage in this type of bibliotherapy improve their mood, decrease anxiety and depression, and are generally better prepared for all that life can throw at them. Increasing your psychological intelligence and becoming mentally strong is not something that happens just because you get older. It's something that must be cultivated and practiced just like a musical instrument or any type of sport. The questions and exercises are important not only because they are relevant to what we will be discussing, but also because they will help you jump in and use the psychological power you'll be learning about.

I highly suggest that you get a journal for answering the questions and doing the exercises found throughout the book. This will give you something concrete to refer to and will allow you to monitor your progress to make sure you're on the right track. I also encourage you to post your thoughts and ideas online on www.TurbulentTwenties.com. Here you can let fellow twenty-somethings know what you are going through as well as read their experiences and the solutions they used for conquering all the challenges they faced after college. You will also find articles about twentysomething life, information on the latest psychological research on our generation, a forum and Q & A section, and links to resources on every aspect of the turbulent twenties. From work to play to dating to personal finances to dealing with stress, www.TurbulentTwenties.com is your one-stop site for everything you'll need help with during your twenties.

you are not alone

If you're reading this now, you may be a college student wanting to know what to expect after graduation so you can be prepared for all that you will face during the turbulent twenties. Or maybe you're a current twentysomething dealing with serious struggles adjusting to life during this chaotic time. You may have tried numerous strategies to cope with this turbulent transitional period. Perhaps you have gone for long walks trying to figure out the causes of your frustration and sadness. Maybe you're constantly talking to a friend or family member or even seeking professional help to talk through your feelings of uncertainty and doubt. Perhaps you've asked your physician for some medication to take the edge off. Or quite possibly, you've done nothing at all simply because you felt incapable of taking any action. Your feelings of helplessness, doubt, and despair may have left you so immobilized that the very thought of trying to get your life together seems far too challenging. As a result, you've been waiting it out, biding your time, hoping that the dark cloud of sadness will eventually fade. If you're a parent reading this, perhaps you're searching for a way to help prepare your child for the challenges of postcollege life. Maybe you're a close friend reaching out to a loved one who is trying to cope with this difficult period.

Regardless of your reasons for reading this book, *The Turbulent Twenties Survival Guide* will illuminate what millions of other twentysomethings are experiencing at this very moment, while providing a road map to postcollege life. If there is one goal of this book, it's to help twentysomethings recognize that the end of college is not the end of life and that each one of us has the power to make our existence significant and meaningful at any age. Precisely to the extent that you attain the proper knowledge and develop the necessary skills, you can achieve all the things you want during your twenties—and beyond.

chapter 1

who are you after college?

What lies behind us and what lies before us are
tiny matters compared to what lies within us.
—Ralph Waldo Emerson

"By the end of senior year, I was so tired of papers and exams that I
couldn't wait to move to a new city, start a new job, and begin my
new life," says Deantha, a twenty-three-year-old from New York.
"But pretty soon I realized that life after college isn't all it's cracked
up to be. It's already been a few years since graduation, and I thought
I would have my life settled, but so much of it is still up in the air. By
now I thought I would be doing all kinds of great things with my life,
but none of it has materialized. I feel really confused about where to
go next, because my life really hasn't turned out the way it was supposed to."

Oprah once said, "Disconnected is the code word for this generation," and if you're a twentysomething who feels lost and

confused, you're certainly not alone. This feeling of disconnect is at the heart of the turbulent twenties, and it all stems from the fact that the moment you step off campus, you are forced to say good-bye to the student identity you've lived with all your life. Suddenly you have to create a new identity to guide you through the rest of your existence. This search for a new vision of self—who you are and who you want to become—is one of the most important challenges that you will encounter during your postcollege years. This is because your deepest vision of self shapes all of the major decisions you will make during your twenties. From what career you choose to pursue, to what type of friends you keep, to whom you fall in love with, to whether you attain the values and goals you dreamed of during college, the positive actualization of these aspects of your life are heavily dependent on the strength of who you think you are and your ability to project the vision of who you want to become into the outside world.

Now, you may have noticed that I haven't said that after college you will experience an "identity crisis." I intentionally avoided this terminology because the identity change you go through after graduation and throughout your twenties is a normal and natural part of this period. Labeling the twenties as a time of crisis stems from the assumption that what you're experiencing is abnormal. But you're inevitably and naturally going to experience confusion, uncertainty, and doubt when faced with the instability of this transitional period. The purpose of this chapter is to help you begin developing the vision of self you'll need to cope with these feelings and the challenges that they stem from.

We begin our vision-of-self by first getting to the bottom of who you are. We start here because before you can move forward in figuring out who you want to become and what kind of life you eventually want to create, it is necessary to develop a solid understanding of who you are. As Nathaniel Branden, author of *The Six Pillars of Self-Esteem* notes, "The turbulence of our times demands strong selves with a clear sense of identity, competence, and worth ... The stability that we cannot find in the world we must create within our own persons" (1995, xi). In today's rapidly changing world, where nothing seems to ever be stable, sometimes the only thing you can count on is your sense of self. By learning how to be more conscious of this aspect of your being, you will begin taking control of the thoughts, desires, and dreams that are inside your mind and will build a psychological foundation for eventually giving them shape, meaning, and purpose in the external world.

your student identity

In order to begin figuring out who you are now, it's necessary to take a look back at the major forces that helped form the vision of self you come out of college with. So let's go back to your first day of school. This is a very important day because it marked the introduction to what may have been the most consistent aspect of your life so far: being a student. Since you were a toddler, the structured and stable environment of school has reinforced your identity as a student by urging you down a detailed educational path and giving you clear, specific goals to achieve. During secondary school you always knew what to expect and how to accomplish all that was set out for you because most things were organized and taken care of by school or your parents. You simply had to show up and do what you were told. If you ever had any problems, you could go to your school counselor, teachers, or your parents for help. There was usually a strong support system available and always a solid line to follow that led you directly to the next phase in life: college.

Structurally, college was sort of an extension of high school, and it provided you with a similar path to follow for success and happiness. Although this varied from individual to individual and certainly depended on whether you went to a small liberal arts school versus a large state school, there are experiences within this variation that the majority of college students experienced. For example, during college your work life centered around four or five classes with a main objective to do well on all your papers, exams, and other coursework. Your work ethic revolved around the idea that if you worked hard and got things done, you would receive the grade or praise you deserved. If you slacked and were lazy, you received something negative, like a bad grade or disapproval from your professor. You never really had to generate a great deal of self-direction because your professors told you exactly what needed to be done—what was required of you was straightforward.

The college schedule was quite flexible, with fifteen, maybe eighteen, hours a week of class and the rest of the week to do whatever you wanted. You had the freedom to do your homework right away or wait till the night before it was due. You had long periods of time to get your assignments done so if one day you were doing your schoolwork and wanted to take a nap, go to the gym, work a part-time job, or hang out with friends, you had the option to put your work aside and do it later. This was the reality of your academic work—clear-cut and straightforward with virtually all the flexibility in the world.

Socially, college supplied you with everything you needed to make friends and provided you with the opportunity to date a wide variety of people. Even before you came to college, the admissions committee had already chosen other students who, although they may have come from different backgrounds, had very similar goals and interests. There were classes, countless organizations, and school events on the weekends where you could meet people, so you never really had to develop major skills for forming relationships.

If there was ever a time you needed help or ran into academic, social, or emotional difficulties, college provided a multitude of people to come to your rescue. There were academic advisors and individual department advisors when you encountered educational problems, residential counselors when you encountered social or living-situation problems, psychologists if you began to feel the pressures of school, parents if you missed home, and a group of friends down the hall for any other difficulties you might encounter.

Together the educational and social environments created an atmosphere that allowed you the opportunity to experience yourself in the most profound way through the expression and actualization of all your distinctive human attributes. That is, it was a place where you could fully exercise your intellectual capacities, your creative capacities, your emotional capacities—and not to mention your sexual capacities. You could be whomever you wanted, because college supplied you with all the opportunities, resources, and structure needed to help you exercise all of your talents and actualize virtually all your goals and desires during this period in life. The avenues of self-expression and self-actualization were open to you like never before, and they were all provided within the relatively safe surroundings of the college campus.

Although the transition to college may have been a bit rough at the beginning, the support and structure provided by school helped you adapt to your new surroundings. Soon you started to get the hang of classes and the new college schedule. Your self-confidence started to rise when you began understanding more of what you read for class, and your intellectual confidence progressively increased as you became more adept at handling the assignments given to you. Perhaps at first you didn't speak much in class, but as you expanded your knowledge and as your speaking skills evolved, you began raising your hand and contributing. The more classes you took, the more familiar you became in the areas you were interested in, and this motivated you to learn more to determine your major and the future goals you wanted to set for yourself. You refined the art of procrastination and discovered how to articulate your thoughts and ideas when you had to write papers at four in the morning or how to pull all-nighters when studying for exams. You found out who to get Biology notes from and what was the best food to eat in the morning after a long night out with your friends.

Eventually you felt like you were part of the college community and seemed to have found a place within these surroundings. You felt comfortable walking through campus and were familiar with where to go for fun, where to go to chill, and where to go for some alone time. Your college experience was a time to begin the process of discovering your passions and was the place to formulate a plan of action that would eventually bring your hopes and desires to fruition.

Although college was not always a smooth ride, and there were certainly bumps along the way, you were in an environment where the fruits of your labors produced quick, visible results. You could be confident in handling virtually any situation that came your way because you knew the college, how it functioned, and knew it would never change. By the time of graduation, you developed an identity with the confidence and capabilities to handle most situations within this isolated environment.

losing your academic self

"When I was in college, I thought I had a pretty good grasp of who I was," says Ursula, a twenty-five-year-old from Boston. "But once I left school it seemed like I had to reinvent myself. I had been so used to being a student that it took me by surprise that you're really not supposed to act like that in the real world. After college, I was no longer defined by what I majored in or how well I did on papers and exams, so a lot of what I did in college didn't really transfer to the outside world. I started to seriously doubt myself because I felt like I didn't know who I was or where I was going with my life. I guess that's just part of the whole process of growing up, but I didn't know it would be so intense. Since graduation, I've had to work hard at figuring out who I really am. When I think back to college, even with all the great things I experienced, my life was pretty restricted. Now I'm just working on finding my place in this whole thing we call adulthood and trying not to let the uncertainty of where I'm going get me down."

Letting go of your former student identity and creating a new vision of who you are is the beginning of a major turning point in your life. After graduation, you are forced to say good-bye to a world you have traveled through all your youth, greeting a new life that is much more complex and in many ways unknown. This simultaneous exit and entrance marks the beginning of the turbulent twenties. To better understand this precarious period of life, let's take a look at it from a psychological perspective.

separation and individuation

If you took a step back and looked at the progress you've made since the day you were born all the way up until today, you would see that the extent of your development has been heavily dependent on how successful you've been at integrating autonomy into your life. That is, the strength of your identity has been dependent on how successful you've been in making the shift from being dependent on others to being dependent on yourself; from relying on external support to becoming self-supporting; from being nonresponsible to becoming self-responsible. The major driving force in this journey toward greater levels of personal autonomy involves the process of emerging from old stages of development and transcending to new, more advanced levels. This process is what psychologists refer to as *separation and individuation*.

To get a concrete grasp of this concept and how it affects you during your twenties, let's take a look at your earliest encounter with the separation and individuation process: your birth. Before you were born, you lived inside your mother and were fully supported by her body. Then, at the time of birth you experienced a separation from your first supporting matrix, the sustaining environment of your mother's womb, emerging into a completely new environment. This matrix shift consisted of suddenly having to exist as a distinct entity in the "outside" world. Your becoming an individual occurred when you began learning the basic motor and cognitive skills that helped activate the process of attaining your sense of physical and personal identity. These first stages of individuation represented the initial steps of your journey toward a greater capacity for autonomy, inner-direction, and self-responsibility.

Now, this is obviously not the place for discussing all the details of this developmental process. However, it is important to understand that this psychological process of separation and individuation is not isolated to birth. In fact, you go through different stages of it throughout your life, particularly right after college. During your transition to postcollege life, you are going through a birth-like type of separation and individuation process as you leave the supportive and structured matrix of college and are thrust into the new matrix of the turbulent twenties. When you depart from the world of college, you are essentially saying farewell to an old level of existence and saying hello to a more advanced level that requires you to confront the challenge of defining yourself in a wider, more realistic context. Essentially, this matrix shift forces you to establish yourself as a distinct, individual entity and develop a more complex vision of who you are within a more advanced, outside world.

a premature departure?

Normally when you separate and say good-bye to an old matrix and individuate into a new, more advanced environment, you leave because you have attained the proper intellectual and psychological (and in earlier stages, physical) skills needed to go on to the next level of development. However, this is not always the case. For example, when a child is born too early, they experience a premature departure from the supporting matrix of the mother's womb (which they have been fully dependent on since conception) and are thrust into an outside world with challenges they are not biologically prepared to deal with. Premature babies often have medical complications such as underdeveloped lungs, no protective layer of fat, decreased body temperatures, and low blood-sugar levels because they have not reached full maturity. It is a biological fact that it is to our best interest to stay inside our mother's womb for the normal pregnancy period because this matrix provides us with the proper environment and necessary nutrients to help us reach the physiological development needed to survive in the outside world.

Well, in the same respect, twentysomethings spend a great deal of money and many years in the "womb" of college to attain the necessary nourishment to deal with the challenges they face during their twenties. However, if you ask any twentysomething if they felt prepared for the challenges they've faced since graduation, you would find that many of them describe their situations as being similar to what happens to premature babies. After recognizing that this new life is not an extension of college, it's easy for twentysomethings to be sent into identity shock. They find themselves facing the reality that their view of themselves, the world, and their place in it has been circumscribed by college and is now inadequate to cope with many of the challenges they face during the turbulent twenties. Soon after entering the working world, graduates quickly realize that who they were in school and what they learned in class is often inapplicable in an environment that doesn't revolve around studying, writing papers, or taking exams. It is this lack of preparation that is making it so difficult for twentysomethings to separate and individuate into their new postcollege lives.

As we will see in upcoming chapters, even though college provides us with amazing opportunities to learn about new ideas and exposes us to things that we wouldn't have experienced outside of academia, the latest psychological research shows that colleges are not thoroughly preparing students for the new challenges of the twenty-first century. The result is a generation of young people who feel a sense of helplessness because their vision of self cannot effectively cope with the new matrix they have just entered into.

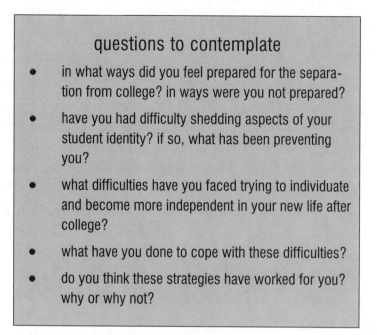

questions to contemplate

- in what ways did you feel prepared for the separation from college? in ways were you not prepared?

- have you had difficulty shedding aspects of your student identity? if so, what has been preventing you?

- what difficulties have you faced trying to individuate and become more independent in your new life after college?

- what have you done to cope with these difficulties?

- do you think these strategies have worked for you? why or why not?

you are what you think

During your postcollege years, the greatest obstacle you will face in achieving what you want out of life isn't a lack of intelligence, talent, or the right situations. What can prevent you from accomplishing all your goals is the idea that what you desire out of life is outside who you think you are and what you believe you are capable of. If you think you're not good enough to do something or that somehow you are not meant to be happy or successful, you will circumscribe who you are and continually prevent yourself from achieving all the important desires that you have during this period in your life. This is quite easy to do after graduation because your confidence in what you are capable of can become seriously weakened. It can suffer a tremendous blow when you realize that you cannot apply much of what you learned in college to what you are actually experiencing during your twenties. That is why it becomes so important to separate from your old student identity, even if you are not fully prepared for your new life, so that you don't continue to have a vision of self that will limit you in accomplishing all that you want during your twenties.

In his book *Honoring the Self*, psychologist Nathaniel Branden writes, "Of all the judgments that we pass in life, none is as important as the one we pass on ourselves, for that touches the very center of our existence" (1985, xi). The reason why this judgment is so important is because what you come to think of yourself after college affects nearly every aspect of your postcollege life. From how quickly you accomplish things at work, to how you deal with your relationships, to how you handle stress, to whether you experience happiness and fulfillment—your response to all the events in your life is shaped by who and what you think you are. Therefore, the esteem you have for yourself is one of the keys to understanding and strengthening who you truly are.

what exactly is self-esteem?

You have probably heard about it countless times, but what exactly is self-esteem? The term may be the most often used, but also the most ambiguous within psychology today. Because people use it in so many different ways, it can be confusing to get a grasp of what it truly means. But self-esteem does in fact have an exact definition, and unless you fully grasp its meaning, it will be difficult to apply it to what is happening in your life during the turbulent twenties. Understanding the precise definition of self-esteem will allow you to distinguish it from other terms used to describe who you are, and by using an exact definition, you can think about it and utilize it with clarity and focus to strengthen your vision of self.

Nathaniel Branden describes self-esteem as having two separate, but interrelated components (1995). The first is *self-efficacy*, which is the confidence you have in dealing with the challenges you face in life. The second is *self-respect*, which is your sense of being worthy of happiness. In other words, your *self-esteem* is the combination of the personal view that you are competent to cope with the basic challenges of life and the view that you're worthy to experience happiness and joy.

self-efficacy: confidence in who you are

You can think of your self-efficacy as the confidence you have in your capacity to be effective and successful in the various areas of your life. You experience your self-efficacy through having a sense of control over your life and confidence in your ability to produce a desired result. For example, when writing an essay in college, a person with high self-efficacy is confident that they will write a thoughtful and insightful paper that will receive a good grade. This person is aware of what she is capable of and is confident in her ability to gather and analyze all the necessary information to put together an organized essay that will clearly express all the points she wants to articulate regarding the topic. A person with low self-efficacy will most likely feel anxious about the essay, even if they know the material, because they aren't confident in their ability to analyze the information and articulate their ideas to produce the result they desire.

Your self-efficacy is rooted in the feeling that you are capable of using your mind effectively to understand reality, are confident in making appropriate choices and decisions in the pursuit of your goals, are able to manage unpredictability and change when events do not go as planned, and are effective in handling the challenges and problems you encounter. Having high self-efficacy means you have a sense of control in your personal world, and the higher your self-efficacy, the greater your chances of succeeding more often than failing. When you have confidence in your capacity to think and act effectively, you trust in your ability to create and achieve what you desire out of life, and persevere with grace under pressure in the process.

self-respect: your right as an individual

Self-respect means seeing yourself as worthy of living life for your own sake and feeling that you have the right to be successful and happy. One way to undermine your self-respect is to let others do your thinking for you. For example, letting your parents or teachers persuade you to become a doctor or lawyer instead of following your dream of becoming a musician or starting your own business reveals a belief that what you think and feel is of no real worth and what others think and want stand above your interests, passions, and happiness. Giving up your goals and sacrificing who you are is the easiest thing in the world to do because, in reality, it takes a tremendous amount of strength, courage, and self-respect to honor your desires, to formulate independent judgments, to remain true to them, and to fight for your goals and passions when everyone else is telling you to be "practical" and stop dreaming. If you don't respect your interests and needs, then there is no reason for others to do so.

Now, I don't mean that you won't benefit from the advice of others and should dismiss the opinions of important people in your life. What you should understand is that, in the end, you are the one who has to live with the choices you make. Therefore, it is you who must take personal responsibility for making the decisions that ultimately determine the course of your life. Having a high level of self-respect means that you feel that you are right as a person, that you are worthy to experience joy, and that you have a right to respect and stand up for your interests and needs.

the highs and lows of self-esteem

There are big differences between people who have high self-esteem and those with low self-esteem. An individual with low self-esteem has the tendency to think and act irrationally, can blind themselves to reality, is fearful of new and unfamiliar people and situations, and becomes defensive when someone challenges their ideas, beliefs, or actions. A person with low self-esteem is a person who feels unable to deal with the challenges of life and believes that they are not worthy of happiness. People with low self-esteem suffer from feelings of inadequacy, insecurity, self-doubt, guilt, and in general are fearful of participating in what life has to offer.

On the other hand, someone who esteems themselves appropriately perceives the world rationally, is more realistic about the events that take place in their life, is flexible and better able to manage change, is willing to admit and correct their own mistakes, and is able to form healthy relationships with others. A person with strong self-esteem is more likely to be creative at work, which means a higher chance of success and financial independence. Strong self-esteem enables your ambition, not necessarily in terms of a career or finances, but rather in terms of who you want to become and what you hope to experience emotionally, intellectually, creatively, and spiritually. A person with strong self-esteem is more likely to form strong relationships with friends, family, and lovers and treat other people with kindness and generosity, because self-respect is the foundation of respect for others.

A good way of thinking about your self-esteem is the experience of feeling that you are competent to cope with the challenges after college and knowing that you deserve to be happy during the turbulent twenties. When you integrate your experience of self-confidence with your feeling of self-respect, you will begin developing a self-esteem that will provide you with the psychological strength to cope with the challenges you face during the turbulent twenties. When you doubt your self-efficacy or self-worth, you will significantly decrease your chances of effectively handling the challenges you encounter in both the external and internal world. A healthy self-esteem is a basic psychological need and when that need is not fulfilled, it can result in feelings of self-doubt, guilt, or inadequacy, and a sense of unworthiness. By developing strong self-esteem, you will be more resilient when confronted with the challenges and hazards of postcollege life and will be better able to cope with the difficulties you face throughout the turbulent twenties.

developing a solid sense of self

Think back in your life and ask yourself if you have ever said, "I can't do it," or "That's just not me." I'm sure every one of us has done this at some point in our lives. What's important to understand about these statements is that whenever you say or think things like this, you limit who you are and what you're fully capable of. You literally attack your self-esteem. If you impose these kind of self-limiting beliefs on your vision of self, you will not allow who you are to extend outside the boundaries you have created and will prevent yourself from doing everything you're truly capable of. Most of the time we attack our self-esteem like this without even being aware of it. However, if you do not make an effort to change these self-limiting beliefs, it will be extremely difficult to create the kind of life you want during your twenties.

eliminating self-limiting beliefs

The first step you can take to increase your self-esteem is to consciously acknowledge the limitations you may be setting on this aspect of your vision of self. To achieve this, what you need to do is brainstorm, trying to think of all the general beliefs you have about who you are, beliefs through which you filter all your experiences. For instance, in many situations you may filter your experiences through general beliefs about yourself such as, "I am so weak," or "I'm a hard worker." In other situations, you may use more narrow thoughts to experience your world such as, "I know nothing about investing my money," or "I am really good at computer programming." The major difference between these two thought processes is that one is generalized about who you think you are while the other is more specific to the situation you are in. This difference can have major consequences on your emotional well-being because more general beliefs can have a major impact your self-esteem. If you're making negative global judgments such as, "I'm not smart," you can create beliefs that may be true in one particular aspect of your life, but not in all the others. For example, it could be that you need to improve certain skills at work, and you are in fact weak in certain areas. This doesn't necessarily mean that overall you are a bad worker. So when doing the following exercise, keep in mind that when you make global negative generalizations, you can undermine your self-esteem and set up a negative belief system about yourself that is not in line with the reality of who you are.

So open up your journal and mark a line down the center of the page. At the top of the left-hand side write "Empowering Beliefs" and on the right-hand side put "Disempowering Beliefs." Now, for the next fifteen minutes, write down all the beliefs you can come up with about yourself and put them into the appropriate category.

After you are finished, take a moment to look over the beliefs you have written down. Circle the three beliefs that you feel are most empowering to you. Ask yourself how they help you. How do they give you strength? How do they enhance your life? How do they make a positive impact on you? After answering these questions, continue to look over the "Empowering" list. As you continue to review it, try to make a conscious effort to strengthen your hold on these empowering beliefs (to "integrate" them into your psyche) by repeating them to yourself. This will increase your sense of certainty that these beliefs are real and true.

Now take a moment to look at the beliefs that you feel are disempowering. Circle the three beliefs that you feel limit you the most. What you're going to do next is begin the process of changing these beliefs by getting down to the root of why you have them. Where do you think these beliefs are coming from? How do these beliefs affect your life? How do they limit you? Do they enhance your life in any way? Why or why not? Do you think they're really defense mechanisms you use to protect yourself from facing scary situations? If so, do they really help you, or do they hold you back? When you begin questioning the validity of these self-limiting beliefs, you will soon see that many of them are not based in reality and are the result of irrational thinking. You can begin changing your disempowering beliefs by deconstructing and replacing them with empowering ones. So take a moment to answer those questions about your self-limiting beliefs. After you've done this, ask yourself, what is their antithesis? What will turn them into empowering beliefs? Write all these answers down in your journal.

silencing the pathological critic

Within each of us there is an inner voice that makes judgments about who we think we are and what we think we are capable of. Whether this voice is positive or negative and how much it affects us depends on the strength of your vision of self. For example, if your self-esteem is low or if you are creating a lot of self-limiting beliefs, your negative inner voice will become more vocal and have much more of an influence on how you think and feel. When this voice starts to interfere with your happiness, it becomes what psychologist Eugene Sagan calls a *pathological critic*. This pathological critic can take on a life of its own during your twenties because the loss of the college structure combined with the instability of the working world can make you feel uncertain and helpless in your new environment. The pathological critic takes advantage of this by constantly putting you down, blaming you for feeling lost.

One of the major ways the pathological critic can make you feel bad about yourself during your twenties is by disrupting the way you think about your experiences during this time. When you are feeling down in the dumps, it is often because your mind becomes overwhelmed by negative thoughts that cause you to view yourself and the world pessimistically. These kind of negative thoughts are usually the result of inaccurate perceptions of the situation, which inevitably result in irrational thoughts and, eventually, negative emotions flooding your mind.

For example, one of the most common experiences that can overwhelm twentysomethings with negative feelings is the idea that they are a failure. So many of the graduates I spoke to said that they had become extremely depressed after realizing that they would not be able to accomplish all the amazing things they dreamed about during college. When they began recognizing that becoming vice president of a company, finding a cure for cancer, or ending poverty are things that cannot be accomplished in a couple of years following graduation, this disappointment can make them feel like failures and fill their heads with a sea of negative emotions.

Dr. David Burns, author of the best-selling book *Feeling Good: The New Mood Therapy* (1999), calls these negative thoughts *cognitive distortions*. During his research with thousands of anxious and depressed people, Burns has found that one of the main reasons you can start to feel so bad about yourself is because of this distorted way of thinking. Essentially, these cognitive distortions are bad habits of thought that you use to misinterpret the perception of what you experience. You experience an event, perceive it through a filter of low self-esteem, mix these perceptions into the stew of negative beliefs about yourself—and emerge feeling rotten. This kind of distorted thinking cuts you off from reality by causing you to not only misperceive yourself, but also the world as a whole. This skewed perception can then cause you to plunge into the postcollege blues because you begin seeing everything in your life negatively, even though in reality there may be nothing seriously wrong.

controlling what you think and feel

To stop the pathological critic, it is essential to always stay aware of the fact that how you feel about yourself is ultimately dependent on how you filter and interpret your experiences. Before you can fully experience virtually any event, whether "bad" or "good," you have to process it within your head first to give it meaning. Therefore, before you can feel something about an event, you first have to develop an opinion of whether it is good or bad for you. What determines your value judgment of any situation you experience is whether you perceive the event rationally or irrationally. If your understanding of what is happening is accurate, then your emotions will be normal, rational, and appropriate (even if they make you feel bad). But if your perceptions contain distortions, then most likely your response will be irrational and more often than not, negative.

You will be better able to manage the way you react to the challenges presented to you during the turbulent twenties if you make a conscious effort to understand how your cognitions work and where these negative thoughts are coming from. By doing this, you will provide yourself the opportunity to eliminate the mental distortions that can decrease your self-esteem and cause you to feel major anxiety and depression. Below are the most common cognitive distortions that the pathological critic uses to try to bring you down.

all or nothing

This destructive cognitive mindset occurs when you fall short at something you're trying to accomplish, and as a result, you make yourself feel like a complete failure. In other words, it is the mentality of, "Either I do everything perfectly, or I am a failure." This self-defeating mindset will cause you needless suffering because you will be unable to live up to the unrealistic expectations you have set up for yourself. It is vital to realize that in the pursuit of your values and goals, effort and struggle are involved—and the possibility of failure. Trial and error are a normal part of the turbulent twenties, and when you do fail at something, you must not think it is the end of the world. Make the decision to get back in the saddle and pick up where you left off.

negative mental filter

This mindset occurs when you see everything in your twenties a negative light, even if most of your experiences are positive. When something bad happens, you dwell on what went wrong, and you perceive the entire event as negative even though only a minor aspect of it may have been bad. It's as if you put on a special pair of eyeglasses that allow you to only see the negative. When this happens, the only thoughts you let into your consciousness are negative, which causes you to feel negative about the whole event. These distorted thoughts can cause you to transform something that is neutral or positive into something that is negative, with the end result being that you blow the negative things out of proportion while minimizing anything that's good.

overgeneralizing the negative

An extension of the negative mind filter is overgeneralizing isolated negative events to the rest of your life. For example, say you ask someone out on a date and they politely decline. You may think to yourself, "Why does this always happen? No one will ever like me. I'm going to be alone for the rest of my life." By applying this one minor incident to your entire romantic life, you can cause yourself a great deal of unnecessary stress.

A good example of overgeneralizing the negative is becoming anxious and depressed because you're unable to find a job you are passionate about (or simply a job that can pay the bills). If you have been applying for tons of jobs and gotten none of them, you might start thinking that you're not worthy of being hired. You think to yourself, either explicitly or implicitly, "I'm just not good enough. No one wants me. My life sucks. I'm a loser." The reality is that the job market may not be that good or you don't realize that college did not fully prepare you with the knowledge and skills needed to land the jobs you may want. It is when you overgeneralize minor setbacks to other aspects of your life and to your vision of self as a whole that you not only cause yourself needless stress, anxiety, and depression, but also blind yourself to opportunities that can make the situation better.

It is also important to note that overgeneralization can work in the opposite direction, where you can overgeneralize the positive and paint an unrealistic picture of yourself and the world. While it's important to have an optimistic outlook on life, the foundation for a healthy positivity is making sure that you have the utmost respect for reality. When you overgeneralize the positive you can pretend to see things that are not really there or create things that don't exist. It's easy to see this happening when people begin dating. There are those times when you make a strong connection with someone you meet and then, based on a few encounters, you overgeneralize this positive experience to that person's whole being and give them qualities that they don't have. In effect, you create a personal fantasy of who you think they are as well as who you want them to be. Then, as you get to know them, their real qualities many times don't match up with the fantasy you have created. Thus, your overgeneralization of the positive clashes with the reality of the person. You're left disappointed because that person is unable to live up to the fantasy you created in your head.

emotional facts

This cognitive distortion is when you use your emotions as evidence of the truth. In essence you take the position of, "I feel, therefore I am," and perceive reality not based on rational thought, but rather by whatever emotion you're feeling at that particular moment. So, if something bad happens such as not getting the job you want, you feel bad and think, "I feel like a loser, therefore I am a loser."

Although listening to your inner signals is important, your emotional response may not be a result of an accurate perception of reality. Relating it to a job situation, you obviously have something of value to offer an employer, and if they did not hire you, it may have very little to do with you personally. Perhaps they were looking for someone with a different set of skills, or the position may have been given to someone within the office and the human resources department was simply going through the interview process because it was company protocol.

But even if you try to be realistic, the pain you feel is real and cannot and should not be denied. Problems develop when you get confused by the strength of your feelings and begin to believe they represent objective reality—"I feel bad, so I must *be* bad." You may be feeling down not just because you didn't get a job, but because you're often telling yourself that you're bad. This is a viscous circle, and it's important to be able to recognize it turning. So whenever you feel anxious or depressed, it's a good idea to check your thoughts and the information available to help understand why you are feeling negative.

jumping to conclusions

Oftentimes you don't take the time to digest all the truths of a given situation and arbitrarily jump to a negative conclusion, even though it's not justified by the facts. A good example is when you try to make assumptions about what others are thinking (usually negative assumptions) and automatically jump to a conclusion, even though you may not understand the whole situation. For example, say you call a friend or someone you've been dating and leave a message on their voice mail. When you don't hear back from them for days or a week, you start to worry. It is extremely easy to jump to the conclusion that something's wrong and try to imagine what is going on in their head. You may think that they are mad at you or don't want to talk to you. Then you start imagining scenes and eventually play out a whole movie (almost always negative) of what the other person is thinking and doing. Then, a week later, the person calls and acts like nothing is wrong. They've been fine, while you spent the week mad, worried, and wondering what was going on. If you go ahead and confront them about not calling, you find out that they never got the message, or they lost their cell phone, or they went out of town for the week. You're left feeling foolish for freaking out about nothing.

Trying not to jump to conclusions and waiting to form an evaluation when you have all the facts of the situation can be quite difficult, but if you can learn to be patient and make a conscious effort to seek out the truth, it will spare you a great deal of needless worrying and frustration.

not stopping the movie

I want you to imagine that you're walking on a beach at sunset. You can feel the soft, wet sand underneath your feet with each step. You can hear the ocean as the water washes up to shore, and you can see the bright orange sun slowly falling into the sea on the horizon. Now let's change scenes and imagine you are sitting down in a doctor's office. The doctor in the white coat tells you to give him your right arm. As you do this, you see him pull out a syringe with a long, thin needle. You watch as the needle inches toward your arm and then finally pricks your skin to penetrate your vein. You then feel the doctor extracting your blood and watch the tube fill up with red liquid. Now before you get too queasy, do you realize what just happened? As you read each scene, you played a movie through your mind based on what you were thinking. You were able to imagine what the sand felt like beneath your feet or the twinge of pain you felt when the needle entered your arm. The image of the beach may have made you feel calm and relaxed, whereas the thought of a needle coming closer to your skin made you nervous and squeamish.

The reason I give these contrasting examples of the beach and the doctor is because I wanted to illustrate the power you have to change the contents of the movie you play in your head. We all have this power, the ability to shift our thinking and get away from a negative focus by making a conscious effort to shift our concentration to something more positive. When you try to make this shift, don't be surprised if the negative movie pops back up in your head again. It may feel out of your control, but when you consistently try to focus on something positive, the negative movie will eventually pop up less and less. What you need to do is reprogram your mind and try to develop a more positive reality filter, which will inevitably lead to a more optimistic sense of life.

unnecessary self-blame

This cognitive distortion is when you start blaming yourself for everything that happens, even though it may not be your fault. Self-blame can become like an itch that you just can't stop scratching, and soon you begin blaming yourself for the things you don't have control over. This habit can blind you to things that are good about yourself and makes you focus on what you don't like about yourself. If you find yourself constantly apologizing for things, then this cognitive distortion may be part of your vision of self. But Homer Simpson put it best when he said, "You can't keep blaming yourself. Just blame yourself once, and move on."

A great way you can increase your awareness of these destructive patterns of thought is by writing about an experience you have had that relates to each one. So, for each of these cognitive distortions, write about a time in which you have fallen prey to this way of thinking. It could be at work, in a relationship, or in dealing with some personal issue. As you do this, think about how you felt and then ask yourself if it was the appropriate response based on what actually occurred.

stopping cognitive distortions

In their best-selling book *Self-Esteem*, authors Matthew McKay and Patrick Fanning suggest that one of the best ways to fight cognitive distortions is by using what they call the *three-column technique* (2000). You can start using this technique by taking a page in your journal and making three columns with the words "Self-Statement," "Distortion," and "Rebuttal" at the top of each. Now, think about a situation that has been causing you to feel bad. This could be something to do with work, a relationship, or something psychological such as your sense of feeling lost—anything that has been making you feel down lately. What you are going to do is write what your pathological critic has been saying about the situation and the

45

cognitive distortions it has recently been creating. Write these thoughts in the first column.

After you're done, examine the statements and see which of the cognitive distortions they fit into. When you figure this out, write the name of the distortion in the second column. After this, write a rebuttal statement in the last column that specifically attacks the cognitive distortion that your pathological critic has asserted. Make sure that your rebuttal statements are strong, specific, and nonjudgmental.

Here is an example of the exercise relating to the job search:

Self-Statement	Distortion	Rebuttal
1. No one will want to hire me.	Mind Reading	There is no way of knowing what they will think of me. It's up to them and all I can do is show them my best.
2. I've already been rejected by so many jobs. I am just not good enough.	Over-generalization	The people who they hired may have known someone in the company even though I was a better candidate. A few rejections doesn't mean that I am unqualified.

By doing this exercise with all of your cognitive distortions, you can get a more accurate picture of what you're feeling, why you're feeling it, and what you can do to change it. This process will help silence the pathological critic so it won't interfere with developing a vision of who you truly think you are.

accepting the self

During the process of eliminating your self-limiting beliefs and stopping cognitive distortions, you will begin to discover things that you may not like about yourself. This is inevitable. But instead of getting down on the not-so-great things about yourself, you can use this new knowledge as an opportunity for change and growth. This is where the process of accepting who you are at this point in your twenties comes into play.

Nathaniel Branden describes self-acceptance as:

> … your willingness to experience—that is, to make real to ourselves, without denial or evasion—that we think what we think, feel what we feel, desire what we desire, have done what we have done, and are what we are. It is the refusal to regard any part of ourselves—our bodies, our emotions, our thoughts, our actions, our dreams—as alien, as "not me." It is our willingness to experience rather than to disown whatever may be the facts of our being at a particular moment—to think our thoughts, own our feelings, be present to the reality of our behavior (1995, 91).

While self-esteem is something you experience, self-acceptance is something you *do*, and it starts with acknowledging the reality of who you are at this moment. When you begin this process, you are not approving or disapproving, just simply accepting who you are at this moment during your twenties. For example, if you admit to yourself, "I don't know who I am," it doesn't mean you are saying,

"I don't know who I am, and that is okay with me." What it means is, "I don't know who I am, and I know it. I may not like it. In fact, sometimes it makes me feel weak, but right now I am putting my judgments and feelings aside and just facing the facts."

becoming aware of your weaknesses

A major element of self-acceptance is increasing your awareness of what you perceive as your weaknesses. So, in your journal divide a page in two, and on the left side list all the weakness that come to your head, leaving a few spaces in between each one. Don't judge yourself when writing these down; just list everything that comes to your head. When you're done, write "Original Perception" at the top of the list. Now take a closer look. How does this list make you feel? Probably not so great. But the truth is that everyone has weaknesses, and there is nothing wrong with it. It only becomes a problem when your pathological critic uses them to bring you down.

Now what you're going to do is revise these weaknesses so that your inner negative voice can't use them against you. On the top of the right-hand column write down "Revised Perception," and next to each weakness, write a revised and more positive version of your weakness. As you do this, pay special attention to the language you use. For example, in the original weakness, did you use negative language such as "stupid," "lazy," or "inarticulate"? If you did, try revisions like, "Need more knowledge in this area," or "Need to be more motivated," or "I need to practice my communication skills." Do you see how just a little change in language can make a big difference in how you perceive who you are?

Now, ask yourself if you are exaggerating or embellishing a negative view of yourself in any way. For example, saying "I'm a flake" is a pretty broad and general statement. It would be much more helpful to be more specific and accurate, zeroing in on what needs improvement. A more accurate statement would be, "Sometimes I am not very reliable." Instead of saying, "I'm too fat," it would be more truthful to say, "I'd like my waist to be slimmer." Do you see how much better it is to use language that is accurate and descriptive when thinking about yourself instead of attaching a negative meaning to your perception?

Lastly, are you being specific about your weaknesses or are you generalizing them? For example, are you saying things like, "I'm *always* late, *never* reliable, *completely* undependable," or are you using specific examples? By using specific language instead of general terms, you will make your weaknesses seem less global and start silencing the pathological critic.

Accepting how you feel about yourself now, during your twenties, does not mean that you deny your desire to change or improve your feelings. In fact, it facilitates change. When you let yourself fully experience how you're feeling, you will understand the truth of your situation and see what needs work. It is not possible to change things that you deny, and by accepting the reality of who you are and what you are thinking and feeling, you will begin developing a stronger vision of self.

the mirror exercise

While working with his psychotherapy clients, Nathaniel Branden (1998) uses a great exercise aimed at increasing your self-acceptance. Take a moment when you are alone and stand in front of a full-length mirror. Now start looking at your face and eventually your entire body. While you do this, start to focus on how you are feeling as you look over yourself. Don't focus on your clothes, your hairstyle, or your makeup. Just focus on you. Is this making you uncomfortable? Is it difficult? After you have done this for a few minutes, take off your clothes and look at yourself again. Pay attention to the feelings that come to your consciousness. Now turn around. Are you hesitant? Do you not want to look at yourself or certain parts of you?

What you probably noticed is that you liked some parts of what you saw, and others you did not like too much. Most people find some parts of their body difficult to look at because they don't like what they see. It may be that you think you are overweight or too skinny. There may be a major scar that you always try to avoid looking at. Perhaps you see signs of aging and are thinking that you don't look as good as you used to in high school or college. It's often hard to stay connected with the thoughts and emotions this kind of experience evokes, and quite often the first impulse is to put on your clothes so you can escape from having the image of your body in your awareness. But keep looking at yourself and, in the mirror, say to yourself, "Whatever my imperfections, I will accept who I am completely, without reservation." As you do this, continue to keep your focus and say this over and over again for a minute or two. Do not rush. Just let yourself experience the full meaning of your words.

During this exercise you may start saying things to yourself like, "How am I able to accept myself completely if I don't like my body?" If this question comes up, keep in mind that accepting means that you experience completely what you are experiencing, without denial or avoidance. It does not mean you shouldn't want to change or improve yourself. Obviously, you probably won't like everything you see in the mirror, but you do have the power to say, "That is who I really am at this moment. I may not like it, but I am not denying it either. I accept who I truly am right now." This respect for the reality of who you truly are is one of the biggest steps you will take in honoring your vision of self.

the psychological evolution of you

Again, I'd like to point out that learning to follow and integrate these types of psychological principles into your life is not an overnight process. It's something that should be seen as a lifelong journey that requires ongoing commitment to self-examination and developing a better sense of who you are. By strengthening your self-esteem, you will begin facing your postcollege life with greater confidence and optimism, and expand your capacity for happiness and fulfillment. In the next chapter we'll move on to how you can use the knowledge of who you are as a springboard for developing the second component of your vision of self—who you want to become during your twenties.

books you will love

Self-Esteem: A Proven Program of Cognitive Techniques for Assessing, Improving, and Maintaining Your Self-Esteem (2000) by Matthew McKay and Patrick Fanning. One of the best books for improving your self-image, increasing personal power, and defining core values. It contains numerous practical strategies that can be used in addition to the ones found in this chapter.

The Six Pillars of Self-Esteem (1995) and *Honoring the Self: Self-Esteem and Personal Transformation* (1985) by Nathaniel Branden. While many books deal with problems of low self-esteem and try to give practical advice about how to increase self-confidence, these books examine the sources and thought patterns that underlie the nature of self-esteem and offers a humanistic approach for exploring the self.

Feeling Good: The New Mood Therapy (1999) by David Burns. A great resource that explains the nature of cognitive distortions and how to use bibliotherapy to alleviate depression.

chapter 2

who do you want to become during your twenties?

Above all; to thy own self be true.
—William Shakespeare

"One of the most difficult things I experienced in the transition from college to the real world had to be the knowledge that from now on, I was in complete control of my own destiny and no one was going to set goals for me ever again in my life," says Abby, a twenty-three-year-old from Philadelphia. "I had accomplished the final milestone in life that your parents hold your hand through. After that, it's like 'whoosh'—the training wheels are off and your parents are no longer running along beside you, but have stopped and are left waving from the sidelines. It's a moment when you can choke and become paralyzed, or you can savor it and use the momentum to propel you into whatever it is you really want to do in life. I realized that my parents were looking to me to see what I would do, when I had always in a way looked to them. Being in this state of complete liberation can be very distressing. It's exactly the infinite number of possibilities presented to you that make it hard to do any one thing (I, of course, was not one of those lucky enough to know way ahead of time what I would want to do with my life). It has been hard to focus. It can be a little frightening and intimidating to think 'Here I am, doing this job, and if I don't do something about it, I will do this for the next forty years of my life and nothing will change.' Knowing that no one will save the day, no one will tell me if I have to do better, get better grades, take harder classes, write a better paper—now it's all up to me. I remember thinking that this was a formidable task in front of me—to set my own goals, to follow through, to exercise an enormous amount of self-discipline, to take my potential future happiness very seriously. It was this aspect of seeing the long, wide road out in front of me, with no one else and nothing else on it except what I chose to put there—that was daunting."

Abby gives us a great analogy to describe what happens to us right after graduation: the training wheels provided by the structure of our educational system are finally taken off and we are thrust into a world where we seem to have complete freedom to choose where we want to go with our lives. This liberation from the constraints of academia can be one of the most exhilarating and exciting aspects of the postcollege experience because we are now free to live life on our own terms. Yet, this state of complete freedom is also at the center of so much of the stress and anxiety that twentysomethings are experiencing today. In fact, the idea that there will no longer be anyone to tell you what to do, no one to make sure you get it done, or no one to come to the rescue if you make a wrong decision can create a sense of panic and nervousness simply because you've never had to act so independently before.

For the most part, up until graduation you relied on your parents and school to show you what direction to go in your life. But after college, you are out on your own, and if you don't take personal responsibility for giving your life meaning and purpose, no one will. As psychologist Mihaly Csikszentmihalyi, one of the world's leading researchers on the psychology of happiness, points out:

> … If we do not take charge of its direction, our life will be controlled by the outside to serve the purpose of some other agency. Biologically programmed instincts will use it to replicate the genetic material we have; culture will make sure that we use it to propagate its values and institutions; and other people will try to take as much of our energy as possible to further their own agenda—all without regard to how any of this will affect us. We cannot expect anyone to help us live; we must discover how to do it on our own (1998, 1).

learning to embrace your freedom

No other generation has had so much freedom to create the kind of life they want than ours. This is our generation's greatest privilege, as well as one of our greatest challenges. While previous generations had only had a few paths to travel down and much of their lives were limited by economic, political, and cultural restrictions, today you can choose from what seems to be an unlimited number of paths. With so many options out there, it can sometimes seem impossible to decide on where you want to go with your life.

"I think finding exactly what you want to do after college seems to be one of the biggest challenges twentysomethings face after graduation," says David, a twenty-four-year-old from Richmond, Virginia. "After coming off the high of praise from their professors, family, and all the graduation speeches, many want to go out and change the world. They feel the need to make an impact on people's lives, but they soon find that it's not as easy as it seems. Some twentysomethings still don't have a clear idea of what they want to do after graduation. Yet there are all kinds of pressures to do something meaningful. It's hard to convince yourself that working at a local coffee shop is putting your college degree to good use. I believe that not knowing what you want to do with your life after college is a problem that most graduates face. Many times we've so many options to choose from and at times, the more options, the harder it is to decide."

But, while finding out what to do with the rest of your life can be nerve-racking at times, many twentysomethings conclude that, instead of fearing the freedom and uncertainty that comes with our postcollege lives, it is much healthier to embrace this new liberation and view it as a chance to explore and discover who you truly want to become. "In college I was pre-med and was all set to go on to medical school, but now I'm actually working at a nonprofit and have absolutely no plans of becoming a doctor," says Emily, a twenty-five-year-old living in Washington, DC. "I had been accepted to medical school senior year, so I decided to take a year off to travel a bit. That was the best thing I could have ever done! I went to Europe and was taken aback by how different things were over there. I was exposed to so much new stuff—art, history, politics—and became fascinated with it all. When I came back, I decided to move to DC to learn more and eventually found a job at a think tank dealing with foreign policy issues. I have spent the past few years trying to learn as much as possible so I can go to graduate school in international relations. Quite a change from becoming a surgeon!

"I realized while traveling that it isn't until you get out there and start exploring and struggling that you finally get a sense of who you are and what you really want. So that is my best advice to twentysomethings out there—go out and explore, no matter how scary it may seem, because you will not get a sense of who you are if you don't. I didn't want to wake up twenty years from now and realize I wasn't where I truly wanted to be because I didn't explore enough before I made the decision to settle down on one road. The other bit of advice is being true to yourself. Sure, it's important to think of the other people you care about and take their opinion into consideration. But ultimately you are the one that is going to be living your life, so you have to be the one who makes the finial decisions."

Like Emily's experience, you can come out of college wanting to become something specific, but once you are exposed to so many new things in the outside world, your view of yourself and the world as a whole expands and, many times, changes the path you had set for yourself in college (and sometimes way back in high school). This can be scary, but not giving yourself the chance to explore can end up locking you into a life that really doesn't fit.

Nathan Gebhard, Mike Marriner, and Joanne Gordon investigate this problem in their book *Roadtrip Nation: A Guide to Discovering Your Path in Life* and found that the reason why so many twentysomethings want to be lawyers, consultants, and doctors is because during college they don't really know that there is anything else out there (2003). The authors traveled across America and interviewed some of the most successful people today, including the chairman of Starbucks, the first female Supreme Court Justice, and CEO of National Geographic Ventures, to see how these people explored and discovered their own paths in life. At the end of their journey they came to the conclusion that our generation is so focused on studying, finding a job, and building their resumé that they lose their youthful curiosity for exploring. Instead, what young adults need to do after college is start focusing on how to express their individuality by searching for a road that accentuates their autonomy rather than sacrifices it.

much easier said than done?

If you're like most twentysomethings, you probably have loads of debt from student loans, earn just enough money to pay for food and your small apartment, and are stuck in a mundane job that provides little challenge or no intellectual stimulation. How the heck are you supposed to explore and learn more about who you want to become in situations like these? Well, just because you can't afford to trot off to Europe or are not working in an exciting and stimulating job doesn't mean that you can't use whatever situation you are in as an opportunity for self-discovery. Even if you only have enough money to pay the rent or are in a job you dislike, you can certainly use the situation you are in as a chance to learn more about the things in life you like and dislike. In all the aspects of your life that you are not satisfied with, ask yourself why you feel that way. Why aren't you happy? Why does the situation annoy you? What is it that you wish was different? What are the opportunities for you to improve or change the situation?

While it can take a bit more effort to learn about who you want to become because you may not be in the most favorable circumstance, by looking for opportunities to learn more about yourself and paying attention to all that you are experiencing, you can use this information to shape what type of life you want to create for yourself during your twenties. As my high school humanities teacher Ms. Jenkins once told our class, "Boredom is a lack of attention," and if you are bored at work, frustrated about your financial situation, or tired of not knowing what you want to do with your life, it may be because you are not using the opportunities in front of you to help strengthen this aspect of vision of self.

questions to contemplate

- how has your life plan changed since you graduated from college?

- what new experiences have changed it?

- have you been disappointed by these changes? why? why not?

- what ways have you explored life after college?

- have you been able to integrate all these new experiences into what you thought you wanted to do during college?

- have these new experiences clashed with where you thought you wanted to go with your life?

- what path are you on now?

- is this the path you want to travel down?

figuring out what you want out of life

"The major stress I experienced after college involved this feeling of, 'Oh my God, now I'm actually supposed to do something with my life! What the hell do I want to do?'" says Ricardo, a twenty-six-year-old from Los Angeles. "I continue to feel scared because of an overwhelming need to come up with some sort of plan for affecting the world. I enjoy my job, make a fair amount of money, and have a lot of friends in the city, but there's a constant pressure that I should be doing more, doing a better job of living up to the promise of my college education. I feel I should be leading mass social movements, changing the world, or at least using my mind to push forward truth, beauty, and happiness. There's a sense that a nine-to-five job is a bit of a disappointment. To whom? My parents? College? Myself, I guess. I think the major stress after college for the highly educated is that we feel like we're suddenly done with the dress rehearsal. Now we're supposed to use everything we've learned and do 'amazing' things. It's often hard to figure out even how to begin."

What wakes you up? What makes you feel alive? What is it that always grabs your attention? What lights you up at your core? These are some of the questions that you must answer during your twenties if you want to solve the problems that Ricardo is talking about. Sure, sometimes trying to answer these questions can be daunting and even overwhelming, but as Ricardo said, dress rehearsal is over, and if you don't make an effort to find out what makes you happy, no one else will. But instead of fearing the responsibility that comes with confronting these self-inquiries during your twenties, it's much more constructive to view this question-and-answer process as an opportunity to figure out what you truly want out of life.

giving shape to your dreams

You gain an enormous amount of power and personal control over your world when you take your generalized aspirations, desires, and dreams and begin defining them into specific goals you eventually want to accomplish. The first step in this process begins by answering the major questions that arise when trying to figure out what you want to do with your life during your twenties. So set aside some time for yourself, grab your journal, and answer the following questions in as much detail as possible.

- what lights you up at your core?

- what are the things that make you feel alive?

- what is it that always grabs your attention?

- what are the things that you are automatically interested in?

- why do these things make you feel so good?

After you find answers to these questions, try to get more specific. For example, begin asking questions like:

- what kind of work relates to these things?

- what are some of the things you eventually want to accomplish professionally?

- where do you want to be professionally and financially in five, ten, twenty years?

- what aspects of your social life do you want to improve?

When you're done, take a moment to look over what you just wrote down. It's a good bet that many of the things you listed are external goals. What you are going to do now is turn your focus inward by exploring what type of person you need to become in order to attain these external goals. You can do this by circling the five most important things to you on the list and for each one, answer the following:

- what do you need to develop within yourself to accomplish what you just listed?

- what new knowledge do you need to acquire?

- what new skills do you need to master?

- how are you going to live today in order to create the tomorrow you want?

When you start exploring both what you want and who you need to become to attain your desires, you will begin acknowledging to yourself that there are things that you're not completely happy or satisfied with. The deeper you get in answering these questions, the more you will begin noticing the difference between where you currently are and where you want to be in the future. This distinction will make you more conscious of the fact that you are dissatisfied with some aspect of your life and it's this dissatisfaction that eventually starts motivating you to begin taking action.

creating structure and direction

One of the most distressing aspects of the turbulent twenties is the loss of the educational structure you lived with almost your entire life. Because it was so easy to rely on school to give you direction, creating the structure and purpose you need during your twenties all on your own can be one of the most daunting tasks you face after college. But as author Mihaly Csikszentmihalyi (1997) has found during his happiness research, your vision of who you want to become is dependent on the structure you give your life:

> Without a consistent set of goals, it is difficult to develop a coherent self. It is through the patterned investment of psychic energy provided *by goals that one creates order in experience.* This order, which manifests itself in predictable actions, emotions, and choices in time becomes recognizable as a more or less unique "self" (23).

As Csikszentmihalyi points out, it is difficult, if not impossible, to begin developing a coherent vision of self without bringing order to your consciousness. One of the most powerful ways you can do this is by learning to set realistic and achievable goals for yourself. This will create the structure missing after graduation and will give you a new path to follow while you try to figure out where you want to go with your life during your twenties.

setting your life goals

If you are like most twentysomethings, you may not know exactly what you want out of life. This is perfectly fine and, in fact, quite normal during this time in your life. If you're still exploring, you can think about your goals in more general terms, like learning about a specific area that interests you or applying for a job in a new field. If you do know specific things you want to accomplish, get ready to write them down.

Take out your journal and review the things you listed from the last section. After you're done, take a new sheet of paper and divide it into three sections. In the first section, rewrite the five most important goals you circled in the last exercise. Then in the next column, write down at least three things about the type of person you need to become to achieve these things. Finally, in the last column write three things you need to change in your life in order to become the person required to achieve all these goals. Be as detailed and specific as possible when you do this.

be realistic

Now, take a look at what you have and ask yourself if what you've written is flexible and realistic or fixed and rigid. For example, you may be thinking of a goal such as, "I am going to apply to business school in six months." This can be a good goal to strive for, but if you know nothing about business, then it would be unrealistic to expect to learn everything needed to submit a competitive application within that period of time. You may have to take a step back and pay close attention to the reality of who you are and where you're at in attaining your goal. So when you set your goals, be honest about what skills and knowledge you have and what you'll need to learn.

divide up your long-term goals

Another thing to keep in mind is that some of your goals may be a bit ambiguous or they may only be achievable far in the future. You will need to break these larger goals down into many smaller tasks that you can achieve quickly and regularly, on a daily or weekly basis. By doing this with all your major goals, you will allow yourself to look ahead to the future while still keeping a strong focus on what needs to be done in the present.

keep your awareness up

Lastly, you will want to keep your goals in your awareness, so put a list of them in a place where you can see them every day. You can keep them in your journal, or you can put them on something you see every day, like your refrigerator or in your car. This will help remind you of what you need to do on a daily or weekly basis to reach those long-term future goals. Keeping them in sight will also allow you the chance to update and revise your goals. You can cross them out as you achieve them and come up with a new list when appropriate. Just remember that keeping your goals in sight will keep them in your mind.

"am I an adult?"

"It's so strange to think that I'm an adult now. I mean, does the fact that I'm out of school and have an apartment and a job mean that I'm grown-up?" asks Silva, a twenty-five-year-old from Atlanta. "When my parents were my age, they were about to get married and buy a house. They seemed to have their whole lives mapped out for them when they were in their twenties. For me, getting married, finding a steady career, and buying a house seem so far into the future. My life seems to be going in a million different directions, but I also don't want to settle down. I still want to try new jobs, travel to new places, and meet many more people, but there's still a part of me that feels that everything is up in the air and I'm not being responsible because I haven't settled down yet. It can be hard because I think society has this specific idea of what it means to be an adult, but I don't think that notion fits well with what our generation is going through."

One of the most ambiguous aspects of today's postcollege years is figuring out what it means to be an adult during your twenties. Twentysomethings told me that part of them feels like an adult because they're out on their own living in their new apartments and working in their new jobs and yet, another part of them doesn't feel quite grown-up because things like having a career, getting married, having a family, or owning a home seem so far off from the reality of their lives.

Psychologist Jeffrey Arnett, the leading researcher on the developmental process twentysomethings are going through today, and Jennifer Lynn Tanner explain in their book, *Emerging Adults in America: Coming of Age in the Twenty-first Century*:

The timing and meaning of "coming of age"—that is, reaching full adult status—is different than it was 50 or 100 years ago, different in fact than it has ever been before. The social and institutional structures that once both supported and restricted people in the course of coming of age have weakened, leaving people with greater freedom, but less support as they make their way into adulthood … More than ever before, coming of age in the twenty-first century means learning to stand alone as a self-sufficient person, capable of making choices and decisions independently from among a wide range of possibilities (2005, 3).

a generation changing the nature of adulthood

Becoming an adult has traditionally been seen as a process of reaching certain events in life, such as graduating from school, finding a career or long-term employment, getting married, having a family, and becoming financially independent from parents. However, if you take a look at the demographics of twentysomethings today, you will see that they are changing the nature of what it means to be an adult during the twenties.

The first and most obvious change is when today's twentysomethings choose to marry. Twentysomethings are continuing to delay a commitment to one person further into their twenties. This is resulting in people having children much later in life as well as buying their home much later. One major reason for this delay is that twentysomethings are staying in college much longer as well as attaining more education after getting their college degrees. They are also waiting longer to settle into careers and are constantly hopping from job to job and city to city to explore all that is out there. As Arnett and Tanner have found:

> Overall, what we see from the demographic outline is that in the past century, the age from eighteen through the mid-twenties has changed from being a period of settling down into adult roles of marriage, parenthood, long-term work, and long-term residence, to being a time that is exceptionally unsettled, a period of exploration and instability, as young people try various possible futures in love and work before making enduring commitments (2005, 7).

we are all "emerging adults"

This has created a new developmental phase Arnett describes as "emerging adulthood." While I mentioned earlier that I do not like using labels to describe today's group of twentysomething's, Arnett's description is different because he is not trying to stamp a catchy label on our generation. What he provides is a term that very much encapsulates the developmental process that twentysomethings go through today as they make the transition into adulthood. When Arnett asked groups of young people, "Do you feel like an adult?" about 60 percent responded by saying, "In some ways yes, in some ways no" (2001). This feeling of being in-between is the result of twentysomethings trying to emerge as adults after college but not quite getting there because of the challenges of the turbulent twenties.

During his research Arnett has found that emerging adults do not use traditional markers of adulthood, such as the attainment of specific things or events that take place at a specific time, to determine if they are adults or not (1994). On the contrary, some of the markers that our generation considers important in becoming an adult are psychological in nature. Accepting responsibility for one's self and making independent decisions are among the top descriptions twentysomethings use. Others markers I've heard twentysomethings use are becoming emotionally secure about themselves, having control over their lives, and being self-fulfilled. As opposed to transitional events like finishing our education, getting married, or buying a house, the criteria that emerging adults are using is much more gradual and psychological in nature.

creating your own timeline

One thing to take away from this discussion on adulthood is that the timeline and criteria for twentysomethings achieving certain markers are in flux. Therefore, if you haven't reached certain markers by a specific point in your life, don't worry about it too much. This time in life is truly about exploring who you are and who you want to become. If you jump into becoming an adult too quickly you can put yourself on a path that is not in line with what you really want out of life. On the other hand, you also have to keep in mind that because we have so much freedom today, our lives are no longer following a predictable sequence of events. With this freedom also comes much more instability and uncertainty. And, as the diversity of paths available to travel down increases, so does the need to take more personal responsibility for which path you choose. In the next chapter you'll learn how to deal with this unprecedented level of freedom and today's overabundance of choice so that you can figure out which is the right path for you.

projecting your vision of self into the future

Who you choose to become is one of the biggest decisions you will make during your twenties. However, one thing I want to stress is that you don't have to decide everything you want *at this moment*. What I really want you to take from this chapter is that this period in life is about looking at all the decisions that you *eventually* need to make. It is much more constructive to think of your twenties as a time to form a vision of who you want to become and then taking the beginning steps of making that vision a reality.

it takes more than self-reflection

As you have seen in these first two chapters, figuring out who you are and who you want to become is not simply a process of self-reflecting your way to a new vision of self. While it's important to your psychological evolution to think about where you want to go with your life, learning to take action by exploring your world purposefully is just as important. There may be no more important aspect of your life to do this in than your work and career. Psychologist Herminia Ibarra explains this idea in the context of finding a career, but her take-action philosophy applies to all the life choices you're facing now:

> We like to think that the key to a successful career change is knowing what we want to do next and then using that knowledge to guide our actions. But change usually happens the other way around: Doing comes first, knowing second. Why? Because changing careers means redefining our working identity—how we see ourselves in our professional roles, what we convey about ourselves to others, and ultimately, how we live our working lives. Career transitions follow a first-act-then-think sequence because who we are and what we do are so tightly connected (2004, 1).

Always keep in mind that self-reflection is not a substitute for actual experience. By both thinking about and testing the many possible futures available to you during your twenties, you will begin painting a clearer picture of the kind of life you want to create for yourself.

books you will love

Roadtrip Nation: A Guide to Discovering Your Path in Life (2003) by Mike Marriner, Nathan Gebhard, and Brian McAllister. Mike, Brian, and Nathan bought an old run-down thirty-one-foot RV, painted it neon green, and hit the road for three months and seventeen thousand miles to explore how other people found their roads in life. Along the way, they interviewed over eighty people, including the scientist who decoded the Human Genome, the director of *Saturday Night Live*, and Starbucks Chairman Howard Schultz. A great source for advice on how to find your path in life. Check out their site at www.roadtripnation.com.

What Should I Do with My Life: The True Story of People Who Answered the Ultimate Question (2002) by Po Bronson. One of the best books I have found that provides insight into answering major life questions. This great book allows you to see the eventual outcomes for people daring to be honest with themselves in answering the major questions that people are facing in the twenty-first century.

Man's Search for Meaning (1997) by Viktor Frankl. One of the most inspiring books you will ever read. Frankl was imprisoned in Auschwitz and other concentration camps for five years, and this is his story of how he struggled and found reasons to live.

Taking Responsibility (1997) by Nathaniel Branden. One of the best books I have read about the role personal responsibility plays in creating happiness in both your life and for the people most important to you.

Working Identity (2004) by Herminia Ibarra. Your life will most likely be filled with many career changes, and this is a great guide on how to smoothly make the transition from one job to another.

Emerging Adults in America: Coming of Age in the Twenty-first Century (2005) edited by Jeffrey Jensen Arnett and Jennifer Lynn Tanner and *Emerging Adulthood: The Winding Road from the Late Teens Through the Twenties* (2004) by Jeffrey Jensen Arnett. Two of the most comprehensive academic books on the developmental process that young people are going through on their journey into adulthood.

chapter 3

how do you know you are making the right decisions?

When you have to make a choice and you don't make it, that itself is a choice.—William James

"I think the hardest thing for me has been all the choices I've had to make," says Leslie, a twenty-five-year-old from San Francisco. "I went to graduate school right after college, so I hit a terrible job market with a bachelors and an advanced degree, about ninety thousand dollars worth of debt, and no real direction. I'm too young for the professor jobs I want (that I went to school for). I've been in a bind trying to figure out where to go and what to do. Which car should I buy (within the one thousand range of course) and where should I live? Should I move into the cheap place in the bad neighborhood, in with a semi-new boyfriend, or take my chances with a roommate? It has been hard to decide which jobs to take, how best to look for the jobs I want, and how to get further training. Mainly, I don't know what to do with myself. I just don't know what path is right and I don't have a lot of room for mistakes because my expenses—medical insurance and student loans—are so high that I have to make a certain amount of money. I feel that I have no room for mistakes (because of my crushing debt as well as incredible fear of failure), yet I also have no idea about and no preparation for making the right choices."

If you took a step back and looked at the time since you were born all the way up until this point in your twenties, you can see that your life has been a journey in the direction of progressively more freedom—that is, a movement toward a life of higher and higher levels of personal choice. As you matured from infant to child, then from child to adolescent, and eventually adolescent to emerging adult, each transition created a wider range of options to choose from while at the same time decreased the number of constraints imposed on your choices. You saw in the last chapter how this freedom can certainly be beneficial to your growth and personal development because it allows you the opportunity to explore all that you want out of life. However, as Leslie explains, twentysomethings can experience major difficulties in dealing with the plethora of new liberties and countless choices that this freedom-filled period creates.

Making all the decisions needed to create the kind of life you want has become far from an easy task for twentysomethings today. In fact, figuring out where you want to go with your life can be one of the most distressing aspects of the turbulent twenties. Psychologist Barry Schwartz has studied this tyranny of choice experienced by twentysomethings after graduation and when I spoke to him, he explained to me, "I found out that the question you don't ask students is, 'What are you going to be doing after graduation?' Although a small percentage of them know, most others are paralyzed because now they can no longer cultivate all of their talents and have to decide on only one. So they end up spending a year to figure out what that thing is and soon one year stretches into five years" (May 31, 2005). In his book *The Paradox of Choice: Why More is Less*, Schwartz has found:

> While students at many colleges are happy to discover a subject to study that not only do they enjoy but that will enable them to make a living, many of the students I teach have multiple interests and capabilities. The students face the task of deciding on the one thing that they want to do more than anything. Unconstrained by limitations of talent, the world is open to them. Do they exult in this opportunity? Not most of the ones I talk to. Instead, they agonize: Between making more money and doing something of social lasting value. Between challenging their intellects and exercising their creative impulses. Between work that demands single-mindedness and work that will enable them to live balanced lives. Between work they can do in a beautifully pastoral location and work that brings them to a bustling city. Between any work at all and further study. With a decision as important as this, they struggle to find the reasons that make one choice stand out above all the others (2003, 140).

Since most of your major life decisions have been structured and narrowed down by the straightforward path of our educational system, facing a new world with a million different roads to travel down can make you feel lost and helpless in your new life after college.

This difficulty is compounded by the fact that in school you were never really prepared to deal with all the decisions you have to make during the turbulent twenties. There were never any classes on how to make good decisions or how to deal with today's overabundance of choice. It still amazes me that there is no real instruction on making decisions in our educational system, even though it's such a fundamental skill that affects virtually every aspect of our lives. As Schwartz told me, "This means for the time being it is up to individuals to pick up these skills on their own." During the turbulent twenties, no one is going to make sure you develop these decision-making skills. It's all up to you, and in this chapter you will learn how to build the psychological intelligence needed to deal with this tyranny of choice and make the right decisions to get what you want from your life.

the costs of opportunity

"Ultimately when you're in school, the answers to questions like, 'What's important to me?' are somewhat, well, academic," says Chris, a twenty-five-year-old from New Orleans. "You're in school. You're taking classes, moving forward in a well-defined system. Then you graduate and suddenly there are a million systems, a million structures to choose from. It's overwhelming. The fact is, life after college is 'real.' You have real decisions to make like: How important is money to me? How much time do I want to spend at work? How important is it that I have a job that I love? How can I stay healthy? Do I want a lot of challenge intellectually? Do I want a varied experience? What kind of risk do I want to take in my life careerwise? Is it important for me to be busy all the time or do I need downtime? How much sleep do I need?"

After college, you're faced with what seems to be an endless array of choices. They can take the form of small questions such as, "Where should I get an apartment?" "Should I buy a car?" or "Should I pay eighty dollars a month for a gym membership?" to tougher questions like, "Should I move to a new city away from my friends and family for that dream job or find a job that is not so great but is near a lot of friends?" or "Should I take that job that pays well but I don't enjoy or take a pay cut and work at a job that I love?" During the turbulent twenties you are confronted with what seems to be an unlimited number of choices, and the fact that you have to deal with so many of them at once oftentimes can be overwhelming.

Barry Schwartz has found that much of the negative feelings that twentysomethings experience while trying to make all these decisions stems from what are called *opportunity costs*. This means that the cost of any option we choose involves passing up the opportunities that a different option would have provided us. For example, whenever you go through the process of making a decision, you first determine the value and quality of each possible choice by comparing it with all the other options available. The problem with this is that when you finally do make a decision, you experience a negative psychological cost because you have eliminated the opportunity to experience all the other options you were looking at. Opportunity costs are a part of every decision because you're choosing between two or more options. The major psychological problem lies in the fact that the more options or avenues you look at, the more opportunity costs you will accumulate, and the greater the intensity of the negativity you feel about missing out on all the other opportunities as a result of the choice you finally do make.

This negative affect can easily be seen in the working lives of today's twentysomethings. After graduation, you are exposed to so many more career options than you knew about during college and after learning about all the options out there, you finally have to decide upon one job to work in. After making your decision, it's easy to begin thinking about all the other opportunities you gave up by choosing that one path. As a result, you can become less satisfied with the decision you came to.

On the flip side, you may be one of the many twentysomethings who can't decide on a career path to pursue and continue hopping from job to job, looking for the perfect fit. But the more you look, the more the opportunity costs pile up, often resulting in major procrastination and indecisiveness as you put off making a definitive career decision. This tyranny of choice can cause you to feel what Schwartz describes as "decision-making paralysis," preventing you from making important decisions that are needed to move forward with your life. In Schwartz's view of what twentysomethings are experiencing after college:

> Everything is up for grabs; almost anything is possible. And each possibility they consider has its attractive features, so that the opportunity costs associated with those attractive options keep mounting up, making the whole decision-making process decidedly unattractive. What, they wonder, is the right thing to do? How can they know? (2003, 141).

One of the most psychologically distressing consequences of all these opportunity costs is the large amount of regret you can feel when you finally decide on one option. Most of us assume that avoiding regret means making sure you've checked out all the other options before making a decision. However, this can create a vicious cycle because the more options you take a look at, the more opportunity costs you begin experiencing. These costs can cause you to experience more and more regret once you finally come to a decision. This can then cause you to start searching for a new and improved choice, starting the process all over again.

when the newness wears off

Another psychological phenomenon that contributes to this vicious cycle of opportunity costs and regret is something psychologists refer to as *adaptation*. In other words, we naturally become accustomed to things and start taking them for granted. For example, think for a minute of how good it feels when you get a new computer, move into a new apartment, or buy a ton of IKEA furniture. You quickly experience a rush of excitement from your new purchase. However, over time the novelty begins to wear off, and your enthusiasm wanes. Soon your new purchase doesn't evoke the same positive feelings that it used to. This is because inside all of us there is a built-in psychological mechanism that does not allow you to sustain the positive feelings you experience about new things you attain.

This adaptation can be seen in the experiences that twentysomethings have in their first jobs out of college. After graduation, twentysomethings can go into the working world thinking that they will be in an exciting environment, working with interesting people, and learning new things each and every day. But soon they realize that the working world doesn't meet all the expectations they had developed while in school. Other times, a twentysomething can land a job that is exciting and stimulating, but inevitably it loses its luster and some level of dullness or boredom begins to set in. In both cases, what do people begin doing next? Looking at job listings and reading all the exciting descriptions. Soon they start imagining the possibilities they could be experiencing in all those other jobs (most of them unrealistic). This then starts the process of accruing opportunity costs because twentysomethings in both groups think of all the things they are missing, which in turn makes them more dissatisfied with their current job (even if it's a good one). They then hit themselves with a double whammy because they are disappointed with the job decision they made and feel regret about the options they didn't choose.

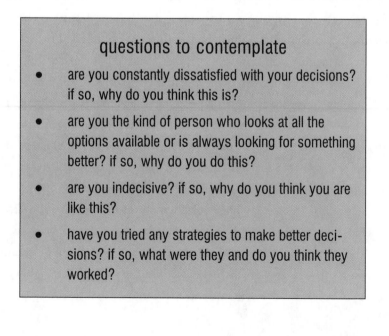

questions to contemplate

- are you constantly dissatisfied with your decisions? if so, why do you think this is?

- are you the kind of person who looks at all the options available or is always looking for something better? if so, why do you do this?

- are you indecisive? if so, why do you think you are like this?

- have you tried any strategies to make better decisions? if so, what were they and do you think they worked?

managing the tyranny of choice[*]

While many times it seems like the overwhelming number of choices today makes it impossible to know if you're making a good decision, Schwartz has come up with a number of psychological techniques that you can use to help narrow down your options and increase the satisfaction of the decisions you do make.

set limits on your choices

One way you can manage an excessive number of choices is by learning to set limits on the options you look at. It's almost automatic to think, "The more choices I have, the better off I will be." However, you have seen how the more options you look at, the more likely you will be unhappy about the choices you make due to opportunity costs and regret. Therefore, it can be healthy for you to set limits on the number of options you look at when trying to make a decision. After discussing this idea with Deborah, a twenty-eight-year-old from Washington, DC, she told me that even though she didn't consciously think about it at the time, limiting her options made her feel more satisfied about some of the major decisions she has made since leaving college. "When I was looking for teaching jobs, I applied to one in DC and one in Virginia, then chose the one I liked better. When I was searching for an apartment, I looked at

---

two places then decided on the one I liked the best. I think because I spent time only looking at a few choices, I've been happier with my decisions because I didn't wonder about other jobs or apartments. Instead, I've spent my time enjoying my current job and apartment and focusing more on the good things about the decisions I made. This is not to say that I won't look for other jobs or a new apartment in the future. It just means I didn't waste time worrying about all the other options out there."

This may sound counterintuitive, but when you learn to restrict your options, you will limit the amount of extra energy you spend on looking at too many choices. By figuring out which choices really matter to you and which are less important, you can focus more time and energy on those decisions whose outcome can bring you happiness and fulfillment. This is not to say that when you are making a decision you shouldn't think about the alternatives. Ignoring opportunity costs can sometimes lead you to overestimate how good the best option is, so it's still good to look at some options—just maybe not all of them. Keep in mind that the more you think about other choices, the more opportunity costs there will be and the less satisfaction you will derive from whatever you finally decide upon.

make your decisions nonreversible

Whenever you leave yourself the option to easily change your mind about a decision, you are giving yourself an incentive to constantly think about all the other options out there, which will cause you to become less satisfied with your initial decision. However, when you say to yourself that a decision is final, you engage in a variety of psychological processes that enhance your feelings about the

84

choice you made relative to the alternatives. Knowing that you're going to stick to that one choice allows you to pour more energy into improving the decision that you've made rather than worrying about changing it and constantly second-guessing yourself.

Now, what if the job you choose to work at is horrible or you got into a bad relationship? Should you make these decisions nonreversible? Of course not. At one point a close friend of mine hated his first job out of college (along with a huge number of twentysomethings), and he told me that looking for other jobs made him feel better about his current one because it gave him hope that something better was out there. So the advice above does not mean that you should stick to a decision even if it's making you miserable. Rather, if the decision you made satisfies you, then stick with your choice and make the best of it.

eliminate "if only" from your vocabulary

Another good technique you can use is eliminating the psychological trap of saying, "If only ..." about your decisions. When things are not going great, it's easy to start saying things like, "If only I had gotten into a better school, I would be a better job candidate," or "If only I had worked on my resumé more or practiced my interviewing skills more, I would have gotten a better job." Sure, it can be good to think over events that have happened to you, recognize what you did wrong, and learn from the experience. However, if you continue to say to yourself, "If only...," you are setting yourself up for an emotional roller coaster and major regret.

When you regret something, it's often appropriate to feel like things would be better if certain aspects of your life were different.

This is perfectly natural and in fact provides a great opportunity to learn from the situation. However, if it becomes so prominent in your psyche that it prevents you from making important decisions in your life, you will have to make a conscious effort to minimize this way of thinking. One way to do this is by limiting the number of options you consider before making a decision. You can also make sure you appreciate the good things about the decision you do make rather than focusing on what is bad about it.

One of the most important ways you can help yourself become more satisfied with your decisions is understanding that any single decision, in and of itself, rarely has the power to completely transform your life the way we sometimes think it will. It's too easy to think, "Everything would have been so different if I had studied harder and gone to my dream school or gotten more experience in college." The reality is that life doesn't work like that. You have to work with what you have now and use the past as fuel to push you forward.

cultivate the habit of gratitude

Schwartz told me that one of best ways you can increase your satisfaction with your decisions is by learning to become grateful about what you have as a result of the choices you've made instead of focusing on what you don't have. When you think about possible alternatives, you can trigger dissatisfaction with the choices you have made. But with practice, you can learn to reflect on the good things in your life, which will make your day-to-day experiences better. An easy way to do this is by keeping a journal at your bedside and each morning or at night write down the things that happened the day before or during the day that you're grateful for. You can write down anything, like a good day at work, a job promotion, or meeting an interesting person, or small things such as a crisp blue sky, coffee with a friend, or a good meal. While it may seem a little silly to do, on a conscious and subconscious level your mind will soon make a shift in what it focuses on, allowing you to keep a greater awareness of the positive things in your life while moving the negative things to the background. A great quote from one of my favorite books, *The Alchemist* by Paulo Coelho, sums it up perfectly: "… when each day is the same as the next, it's because people fail to recognize the good things that happen in their lives every day that the sun rises" (1995, 29).

bringing emotional intelligence to your decisions

During my first week in college, I met Steve. He was valedictorian of his high school and a math wiz who was just a few points shy of getting a perfect SAT score. Steve was one of the most intelligent people I had ever met and yet, at the end of the first semester, he was on probation for nearly flunking two of his classes. The reason Steve had done so poorly in school was because he had spent most of his semester hanging out with friends, drinking, getting high, and sleeping until one or two in the afternoon. At the end of the year, he had to leave our school for a year and take classes at a community college before coming back. I still don't know if he ever graduated.

Whenever I thought about Steve, I always used to ask myself how someone with such a high IQ could act so dumb. Why did he have so much trouble making good decisions? I soon found the answer in Daniel Goleman's groundbreaking book *Emotional*

Intelligence: Why It Can Matter More Than IQ (1995). What Goleman has found during his years of intelligence research is that things like IQ, the ability to get a high SAT score, or good grades are not always the best ways to predict who will succeed in life. This is not to say that there isn't a relationship between IQ, SATs, grades, and future success. There certainly can be. However, more and more research continues to show that they aren't the only factors involved, says Karen Arnold, professor of education at Boston University who tracks valedictorians. "To know that a person is a valedictorian is to only know that he or she is exceedingly good at achievement as measured by grades. It tells you nothing about how they react to the vicissitudes of life" (Johnson and Murray 1992).

As Arnold and many other psychologists have known for quite some time now, being smart by traditional academic standards does not always mean that a person will make good decisions. As Goleman explains:

> Academic intelligence offers virtually no preparation for the turmoil—or opportunity—life's vicissitudes bring. Yet, even though a high IQ is no guarantee of prosperity, prestige, or happiness in life, our schools and our culture fixate on academic abilities, ignoring *emotional intelligence*, a set of traits— some might call it character—that also matters immensely to our personal destiny. Emotional life is a domain that, as surely as math or reading, can be handled with greater and lesser skills, and requires its unique set of competencies. And how adept a person is at those is crucial to understanding why one person thrives in life while another of equal intellect, dead ends ... (1995, 36)

the importance of emotional awareness

What if I told you that you cannot make a rational decision without using your emotions? This seems like an illogical statement because people typically think of emotions interfering with our ability to make good, rational decisions. However, research by Dr. Antonio Damasio, a neurologist at the University of Iowa College of Medicine, has shown that it is virtually impossible to make a good decision if you do not have adequate awareness of your emotions (1994). The evidence for this comes from Damasio's research on patients with damage to the prefrontal-amygdala-circuit, the emotional part of our brain that stores the likes and dislikes you acquire over the course of your life. Damasio has found that people with damage to this area of the brain have seriously flawed decision-making capabilities. But what is extremely interesting about this is that these same patients show no deterioration in their IQ or cognitive ability. Even though their intellectual faculties are intact, these individuals continue to make terrible choices in their personal and professional lives. This has led Damasio to suggest that the reason these people make such disastrous decisions is because they have lost the ability to learn emotionally as well as gain access to old emotional memories.

When access is cut off to the amygdala, things that normally trigger an emotional reaction don't because there is no longer any access to the "warehouse" that holds all the emotional memories associated with similar events in the past. As a result, patients with damage to this area have forgotten all the emotional lessons they have learned during their lifetime. So when they are presented with something that normally elicits an emotional reaction, such as a favorite TV show or a person that they strongly dislike, it no longer triggers excitement or aversion—it is simply neutral.

the importance of knowing your values

The powerful role that emotions play in making rational decisions has also been demonstrated in Damasio's study of Elliot, a patient who had a tumor removed from behind his forehead. Although his surgery was seen as a success, it caused a drastic change in Elliot's personality. Intellectually, he was as bright as ever, but he was unable to use his time efficiently, would get lost in minor details, and seemed to have lost all sense of priority. As a result, he could no longer hold a job, his wife left him, and he squandered his savings.

Elliot went through extensive intellectual testing and Damasio found nothing wrong with his mental faculties. His logic, memory, attention, and all other cognitive abilities were completely intact. But Damasio noticed that Elliot was virtually oblivious to his feelings about what had happened to him. If you asked Elliot about his surgery and the difficult events that happened to him afterwards, he would discuss them without emotion. There was no sign of regret, sadness, frustration, or anger in his tone. This was because the surgery had severed the connection between the amygdala and its related circuits—that is, the emotional brain from the intellectual, thinking part of the brain.

While Elliot was still able to think about every step in a decision, he was unable to actually make a decision because he couldn't assign *value* to the different possibilities. To him, every option was neutral. Because of this lack of awareness about his own feelings, Elliot's reasoning and decision-making abilities suffered. This could be seen in even the simplest of decisions, such as choosing a time and date for an appointment. Elliot could find rational arguments for and against every date and time, but he was unable to choose one simply because he lacked any sense of how he felt about any of them. What Elliot's experience demonstrates is that decisions cannot be made simply through rational analysis. They require an awareness of your feelings and your ability to use that knowledge to make intelligent choices.

using your gut

Emotions are what usually point you in the right direction, and by listening to your gut you can use this information to begin thinking long-term about a decision and eventually use logic to ensure that the path you finally take is correct. This is especially relevant today, as we confront a world of virtually unlimited choice after graduation. Deciding on things like where to live, what kind of job you want, what career to pursue, or who to date or marry are all decisions you must confront during your twenties, and it is the emotional learning that life has given you (such as a bad job experience or a painful breakup) that can streamline the decision-making process by eliminating some options and highlighting others.

Developing your emotional awareness is extremely important to the decisions you make during your twenties because you use it to navigate through the array of options in today's overabundance of choice. Although you might usually think of strong feelings as wreaking havoc on your ability to reason, your inability to be aware of what you feel can be just as disastrous. By using your inner signals to help you pare down the numerous choices you have throughout your twenties, you can add emotional intelligence to your IQ and reasoning abilities to help you make better decisions about where you want to go during your twenties.

who are you listening to?

Throughout your youth you have used external signals to direct most aspects of your life. Your parents told you how to behave, the educational system showed you which direction to travel, and a multitude of other people were always telling you the best way to live your life. The potential problem with this is that the feelings for what you truly wanted may have been drowned out somewhere along the way. As a result, the act of listening to your deepest emotions and desires— your inner signals—can be a foreign experience after graduation because you have always listened to the advice of external sources and structures to show you what to want, what to do, and who to be.

Listening to so many external prompts throughout your life can lead to focusing on external achievements, such as finding an exciting and high-paying job, buying a nice car, or living in a big house. These are all well and good, but it's also important to become skillful and accomplished in the development of your inner world and of your awareness of all of your needs, desires, hopes, dreams, and frustrations.

If you become out of touch with your emotional self, you can also become blind to important aspects of the external world, failing to see opportunities for growth and development in your environment. For example, if you deny your desire for greater autonomy in your job, you can become oblivious to opportunities that give you more responsibilities and a chance to improve your skills. If you reproach yourself for feeling lonely and deny the desire for friendship and a sense of community, you can become oblivious to offers of companionship from people who care about you. If you deny the reality of how hard it can be to redefine your vision of self during the turbulent twenties, you can blind yourself to the possibility that you are living in the past.

Your emotions are a part of reality, just like a job, apartment, or friends, and when you make a conscious effort to become aware of what you're feeling—even if it is embarrassing or scary—you are then able to own your feelings and bring them into contact with the rest of your knowledge. This will eventually help you to process these emotions rationally and learn from them for future development. Self-examination and self-acceptance are essential components of personal growth, and if you don't allow yourself to fully acknowledge, accept, and experience your emotions, then you run the risk of burying important needs and wants deep within and severely restricting the expansion of your vision of self.

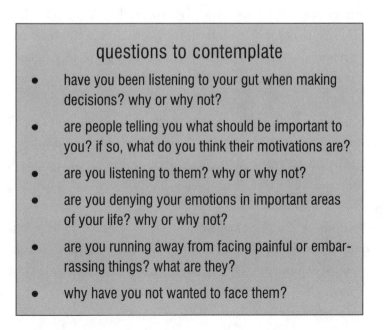

questions to contemplate

- have you been listening to your gut when making decisions? why or why not?

- are people telling you what should be important to you? if so, what do you think their motivations are?

- are you listening to them? why or why not?

- are you denying your emotions in important areas of your life? why or why not?

- are you running away from facing painful or embarrassing things? what are they?

- why have you not wanted to face them?

a personal account

When I came out of college, I thought I had everything figured out. I was a psychology major, had fallen in love with the field, and planned to make a career out of it. In college, I had done a great deal of research on depression and started my first book on the antidepressant effects of exercise (called *Feeling Good for Life*, 2001) during my senior year, so I was deeply immersed in the subject. The plan after graduating was to take some time off, get more psychology experience, finish up my book, and then go to graduate school in clinical psychology. I wanted to become a professor with the possibility of opening up my own practice on the side.

It seemed like a solid path to follow, but as soon as I graduated I became exposed to many more things than I expected—most of which I was never aware of in college. My world really opened up because in college all I knew was psychology; I hadn't really allowed other things to penetrate my consciousness. As I was exposed to different experiences and ideas, my interests began to widen and change. However, I did not fully integrate all I was learning because it didn't fit into the clinical psychology plan I had set in school.

Over the next few years I finished my first book and thought I wanted to pursue this area of research for the rest of my life, so I decided to apply to graduate school for clinical psychology. I applied in the fall, checked this off my life plan, and went to Barcelona to study abroad for a semester.

I had never gotten a chance to study abroad in college due to other commitments, so I figured this was the perfect time for me to go because I would learn a lot, have a great time, and then come back to head off for graduate school. Little did I know how being away from the structure of my life would drastically change my idea of the world and my place in it. While I was in Barcelona, the second book and graduate school seemed like a distant memory as I became exposed to so many new things in a completely different world. I still thought about graduate school every so often, but only when people would ask me what I was going to do when I got back to the states. Then came the day that would make me fully aware of how unconscious I had actually been of my emotions.

I was in a café starting to formulate the ideas for *The Turbulent Twenties Survival Guide* when I received a call from my mom. She began the conversation by telling me that she had some bad news and then told me that I had been rejected from grad school. In thinking back to that conversation, what was so striking about that moment was my initial reaction to the news. I didn't experience shock, nor did I feel any type of devastation; I simply felt indifference. The first thing I actually did was comfort my mom because she seemed to be so sad that I didn't get in. I told her not to worry because I would figure something out and then I got off the phone. I sat back down at my table and with a small shrug and a sip of my cooling coffee, thought, "That sort of sucks"—and continued on with my writing.

Over the next few days I had to remind myself that I needed to think about what had just happened. So I set some time aside to be by and with myself so I could take a step back to figure out why I hadn't reacted as negatively as I thought I should have about not achieving this major step in my life plan. I went home and laid down on my bed, and as I relaxed my body, I started saying out loud everything I was thinking and feeling about what had happened. As I began acknowledging and experiencing all of my emotions, I soon realized that I had decided a long time ago that my interests and passions had changed because of the new things I had been exposed to, and graduate school for clinical psychology really wasn't that important to me in the long run for many of the new goals I wanted to accomplish. The problem was that I had blocked myself from becoming fully conscious of the fact that I was feeling like this.

What actually happened was that on a deeper level, I had known a long time ago that the clinical psychology path was not completely right for me. But I continued to ignore my emotions and the signals my inner self was giving me because I had formed a rigid path in college and acted stubbornly not to deviate from it. The new things I was experiencing were extremely interesting and exciting, but they were not part of my master plan, so I didn't fully integrate them into my life. I can even recall that back when I was filling out the application to graduate school, there was this little voice inside my head saying that researching and writing about exercise, nutrition, obesity, and depression was fun, but it wasn't what I wanted to do forever. These issues were no longer waking me up and getting me as excited as they used to. In hindsight, I now see that I was trying to force myself to feel something that I couldn't. I continued to justify staying on this old path by saying that I would just try to expand my interests and incorporate these new things while in clinical psychology school. However, the reality of the situation was that if I had gone ahead to graduate school in clinical psychology, it would have boxed me in. I would have spent the majority of my time researching topics that I wasn't truly interested in, and this would have severely limited my personal development. Somewhere along the way I had become unconscious of my emotional self and what I truly felt was right. I was no longer listening to my inner signals telling me what my passions really were simply because I had formed a rigid plan in college about what I wanted to do for the rest of my life and was determined to stick with it.

Today, I am very thankful that I didn't get into graduate school because I would be doing something I wouldn't be completely interested in and wouldn't be as happy as I am now. Sure, it would have provided me security and purpose for five years and I would have had a set career path, but I would have also been stuck in something that would have limited me in the things I truly want to accomplish now that I've had time to explore other things in life. I now see that when we set rigid plans at such an early age, it can be difficult to move away from them, even if our inner signals are screaming at us to try something new or drop something old. I still am going to pursue psychology, just not the clinical route. I'm also going to incorporate the things I've learned outside of psychology to help crystallize the path I truly want to take.

be true to your inner self

It is extremely common to come out of college wanting to become something specific then change this idea once you're exposed to so many new things in the outside world. After graduation, the vision of self you hold and the perception of the world as a whole expands and many times alters the path you have set for yourself during college. This change in your master plan is a normal part of individuating into your new life during your twenties and doesn't have to be seen as a source of stress. You can reframe it as an opportunity for exploration of what you want and who you want to become. Always remember that you have the power within to change the path you want to take.

During the course of writing of this book, one of the most important things I've discovered is that our generation feels pressured to have things figured out by the time they graduate. As a consequence, they tend to see college as the end of learning when in reality, it's just the beginning. If you do not view your life after college as a time of exploration and self-discovery and don't listen to your inner desire to learn, understand, and integrate all the new things you experience after graduation, then you run the risk of limiting the development of your vision of self and moving on to paths that may not be completely right for who you are and where you truly want to go. This is why it's so important to learn to listen to your emotions in making those decisions on where you want to go with your life.

being by and with yourself

As I illustrated earlier, one of the best ways to get in touch with your inner signals is by taking time to be *by* and *with* yourself, allowing everything you are thinking and feeling to be experienced. Whenever I feel troubled about something, I go somewhere I can be alone, sit in a comfortable chair or lie down on my bed, and say out loud everything I am thinking and feeling. I relax my entire body and allow myself to acknowledge *and* really experience all of my emotions. I stress the importance of doing both because it's one thing to say out loud what we are feeling, but it's quite another to actually experience it. It's not until you allow yourself to fully experience what you're feeling, even if it's frightening, that you will be able to fully discharge your emotions.

Lots of people try to keep their emotions bottled up because they don't want to show others what they are truly feeling or don't want to experience the negativity brought about from their current emotional state. To them, it's easier to repress their feelings. But your feelings don't disappear just because you try to ignore them. When you try to do this, you bury your emotions deep into your subconscious where you have no control over them. When you do allow yourself to fully acknowledge and experience your emotions, you are able to learn more about them, understand them, and eventually own them. This way, you are the master of your emotional state and not a slave to how you're feeling moment to moment.

When you acknowledge and accept how you are feeling, it does not mean that your emotions have the final say. For example, sometimes you may not feel like going into work in the morning. What you can do is acknowledge how you're feeling, experience it fully, accept it—and then move on. By doing this, you will go to work with a consciousness that is much clearer because you have not started your day out by denying how you are truly feeling.

books you will love

The Paradox of Choice: Why More Is Less (2003) by Barry Schwartz.
One of the most illuminating works on the importance of bringing greater awareness to the decisions we make in today's overabundance of choice. Whether we are choosing a job, career, whom to marry, or a cell phone, Schwartz shows that more is not always better and the bewildering array of choices today can actually cause us to become less satisfied with our choices.

Emotional Intelligence: Why It Can Matter More Than IQ (1995) by
Daniel Goleman. A book that I believe every twentysomething should read. This book will provide you with the foundation for everything that college did not teach you and will enhance every single aspect of your life.

chapter 4

how do you conquer the postcollege blues?

Happiness depends on ourselves.—Aristotle

"During my first year after college, I fell into a really deep depression," says Jody, a twenty-four-year-old from Portland. "I decided to go out west because I got offered a job I couldn't pass up, but soon after I got there, I became sad and lonely. My job wasn't what I expected it to be and I really started to miss college and all my friends. My life had changed so much and I felt like I didn't have control over it. I still feel pretty lost because I don't exactly know what I want to do with my life yet, but I'm hoping that I'll figure that out soon."

One of the most alarming discoveries I came across during my research of the turbulent twenties was that experiences like Jody's are extremely common among twentysomethings today. So many graduates I spoke to told me that either they had become depressed or knew of fellow twentysomethings who had developed major depression. Along with depression, many spoke about feeling extremely nervous about how their life was unfolding because they didn't know what the next step was and felt like they were simply wandering through their twenties.

What compounds this worry and stress is the assumption that what these twentysomthings are experiencing is abnormal. But if you are feeling anxious, helpless, or depressed, you certainly aren't alone. Because of the nature of this transitional period, it is extremely common to struggle with an array of negative emotions that arise from all the challenges you face after college. However, just because you're susceptible to these feelings doesn't mean that you have to let them take over your life. There are proven strategies you can use to beat the postcollege blues, and what I will show you in this chapter is how to use these clinically tested methods so that you can begin taking control of your emotional health.

the two forms of the postcollege blues

As I spoke with both younger and older twentysomethings, I found that there are two distinct times during the turbulent twenties that graduates are most susceptible to the postcollege blues. The first is right after graduation, and the reason why this is such a vulnerable period is because there's never been any other time in which so many aspects of your life change so quickly and drastically. From work and your career, to your finances, to your relationships, to coping with creating a new vision of self, so many parts of your life can be up in the air. What's worse is that you have to attend to them all at once, which can overwhelm you and cause you to feel like you don't have any control over the important areas of your life.

The experience of this first form of the postcollege blues is remarkably similar to a clinically diagnosable condition that many women go through after giving birth: postpartum depression. The symptoms for this condition are:

- difficulty concentrating or making decisions

- feelings of worthlessness or guilt

- focusing on failure at motherhood

- excessive anxiety

- lack of confidence

- feeling of being overwhelmed

- sadness

- loss of interest in normal activities

- tiredness

- feeling like you're not good enough

- impaired concentration or memory

- inability to cope

- despondency or despair

- hopelessness

When you compare the list above with the personal accounts you've read so far, you can see that what twentysomethings are experiencing during the postcollege blues is remarkably similar to what women experience during postpartum depression.

Aside from the biological changes a woman goes through after giving birth, one of the reasons why women can develop postpartum depression is because they find themselves having to take on new roles, such as mother and caretaker. Since these roles are often not well defined, women can go into motherhood without a clear idea of what the role actually entails and feel lost while trying to be a "mother." Well, we have seen that a similar phenomenon occurs when twentysomethings are forced to shed the role of student to take on new roles that fall under the umbrella of the often ambiguous term of "adult."

New mothers can also develop major feelings of anxiety and self-doubt because of the unrealistic expectations they can form about being a perfect mother. Mothers report that the idea of failing to do a good job raising their children can be terrifying to them. Similarly, twentysomethings have high expectations about what they want to accomplish after graduation and can eventually develop feelings of self-doubt after realizing how unprepared they are to deal with many of the new challenges they face while trying to achieve the goals they set for themselves during college.

New mothers report that one of the major worries they have after giving birth is the new financial burdens and economic insecurity that can occur during motherhood. Money also has a major impact on the lives of twentysomethings because many of the jobs twentysomethings work in after college do not pay that well. Combine this with loads of student-loan debt and it's easy to see how twentysomethings can feel a great deal of stress and anxiety when thinking about their finances.

Lastly, the types of interactions that mothers have with their family and friends can change, and if new mothers don't have the support needed for this transition, they can develop a greater risk for depression. This is the same for most twentysomethings who see the support systems they were accustomed to for years disintegrate after college.

The second point in which twentysomethings can develop the postcollege blues is during the mid-to-late twenties. It is at this point that it dawns on them that five or more years have passed since graduation and their life is not where they thought it would be when they planned it all out during college. For example, when you were younger you most likely thought that by your mid-to-late twenties you would have a great-paying job that you loved, a defined career, a plan to change the world, a great group of friends, a serious romantic partner or even a spouse, a house of your own, and a generally settled life. But as we discussed in chapter 2, if you're like most twentysomethings, you have only a few, if any, of these things in your life. Most likely, the job you are in is not your dream job, you are not settled in any type of career, not married (or have not even met anyone who comes close to that point), renting a small studio that takes up half your paycheck or living with a group of other twentysomethings, can't even come close to affording a house, not making much money and quite possibly, living back home with the parents. At this point you also have to accept the fact that you cannot change the world so easily or accomplish all that you want as fast as you could during your academic years.

One of the most powerful elements of both forms of the postcollege blues is that during the turbulent twenties you begin coming face-to-face with your mortality. If you are a twentysomething right out of college, it slowly dawns on you that the old way of life is gone forever, and you will never be able to relive your undergraduate years. While some of the twentysomethings I spoke to were going to graduate school, every one of them said it just wasn't the same as undergrad. For those of you who are in your mid-to-late twenties, the dread of turning thirty can make you feel like another part of your life is over and there is no going back. When you were in your teens and turned twenty, you probably never thought, "I'm going to miss my teens so much!" At that time you were in the midst of college, having a great time, so it really wasn't a major turning point in your life. But ask any twentysomething who is about to reach thirty, and they will tell you how a feeling in the pit of their stomach can start to grow as they begin realizing that they are getting older and will never be able to relive their twenties. In both forms of the postcollege blues, the fact that time is passing by becomes a much more prominent fixture in your mind and you begin understanding that there are things in life that you will never be able to experience again in the same manner.

a generation plagued by helplessness

Suppose you took a rat and put it in a steel cage. In this cage there is a floor that can produce a mild electrical shock whenever you press a button. You then press the button and give a shock to the rat. As soon as you do this, the rat begins squealing in pain, starts tearing at the floor, and tries to climb the walls to escape. You end the shock after five seconds and eventually the rat calms down. But then, a minute later, you shock it again for five seconds, and the rat responds the same way. Well, if you were to repeat this eighty times, by the end of the final session you would not get a rat that is yelping or trying to climb the walls. What you would have is a rat that huddles in the corner and does nothing to try to stop or escape the shocks.

Now, if you were to take the same rat that you just shocked and put it in a cage where it was able to turn off the shock by simply running to the other side, you would see that the rat doesn't make any particular effort to try to stop the shocks. It would just sit there listlessly and take the pain. Why wouldn't the rat try to stop or prevent the shocks? It's because whenever you expose animals to situations that are uncontrollable, something dramatic happens to them psychologically: at some level, they assume that nothing they do will stop the pain, so they decide to do nothing.

Psychologist Martin Seligman, former president of the American Psychological Association and a professor at the University of Pennsylvania, was the first person to do these types of experiments, and what he uncovered was that this psychological change of the rat is not dependent on the actual pain from the shocks it receives, but rather on whether the situation it is in is perceived as uncontrollable. During this same line of research with dogs, Seligman found, "When shock is inescapable, the dog learns that it is *unable* to exert control over the shock by means of any of its voluntary behaviors. It expects this to be the case in the future, and this expectation of uncontrollability causes it to fail to learn in the future" (1993, 20). Seligman describes this behavior as *learned helplessness*, and what he has discovered is that this same type of reaction experienced by rats and dogs is also found in humans during situations we believe are uncontrollable.

Twentysomethings today can develop this kind of learned helplessness because it can seem like you don't have control over important aspects of your life. Because of a perceived instability in your life, you can start forming the belief that your life is uncontrollable and assume that this is how it will be in the future. And even though you may not actually be helpless in the literal sense, your perception of helplessness can make you believe that you're unable to effectively cope. These feelings of helplessness can be focused on specific situations, such as a feeling like you are not able to find a good job, you can't find someone good to date, or you have no idea who you want to become during your twenties. Other times it can be more general, such as feeling like you don't fit into major life roles like worker, lover, or friend.

the price of high expectations

After graduation you have the freedom to be the master of your own fate and can choose any direction you want to go with your life. Because you are now able to exert more control over your life than ever before, you may feel like you should be able to protect yourself from feeling helpless. After all, it's only in situations where you have no choice that you become vulnerable to learned helplessness, right? Well, as we saw in chapter 3, just because you have more choice does not necessarily mean that you are always better off. In fact, today's overabundance of choice can actually plunge you into the postcollege blues.

Psychologist Barry Schwartz believes that this is because of two major factors. First, because we have grown up in a time of increased choice and higher levels of experienced control, there has also been an increase in *expectations* about control. As Schwartz explains, "We should be able to find education that is stimulating and useful, work that is exciting, socially valuable, and remunerative, spouses who are sexually, emotionally, and intellectually stimulating and also loyal and comforting ... With all the choice available, we should never have to settle for things that are just 'good enough'" (2003, 210). Not only have we grown up expecting perfection in all external things, but we also expect it from ourselves. We expect to be able to manage every aspect of our life and when we fail or seem to lose control, we blame ourselves intensely, making us susceptible to the postcollege blues. As Schwartz has found in his research, "Unattainable expectations, plus a tendency to take intense personal responsibility for failure, makes a lethal combination" (214).

maximizers vs. satisficers

One possible factor in determining whether you will develop this kind of learned helplessness is whether you are a maximizer or a satisficer. A maximizer is someone who strives to make the best possible choice in every instance while a satisficer simply looks for the choice that is "good enough." For example, if a maximizer went shopping for a new laptop, he would try to look at as many models as possible and do intensive research on all of them to figure out which is the best possible choice. But as we talked about in chapter 3, the more choices he looks at, the more opportunity costs he will acquire, and the greater the decrease in happiness that person will derive from the decision they finally do make. On the other hand, when a satisficer goes shopping, she has a certain set of parameters to judge her choices by, and when she finds the laptop that satisfies those parameters, she stops the computer search and buys the laptop that fits her needs.

What Schwartz has found is that satisficers, in general, are happier with their decisions (and with life as a whole) than maximizers. As Schwartz explains:

> ... maximizers are prime candidates for depression ... we have found a strong positive relation between maximizing and measures of depression. Among people who score highest on our Maximization Scale, scores on the standard measure for depression are in the borderline clinical depression range.

With respect to young people today, Schwartz goes on to say:

> We find the same relationship between maximizing and depression among young adolescents. High expectations and taking personal responsibility for failing to met them can apply to educational decisions, career decisions, and marital decisions, just as they apply to decisions about where to eat ... If the experience of disappointment is relentless, if virtually every choice you make fails to live up to expectations and aspirations, and if you consistently take personal responsibility for the disappointments, then the trivial looms larger and larger, and the conclusion that you can't do anything right becomes devastating" (2003, 214).

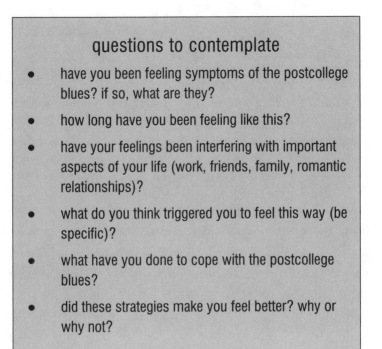

questions to contemplate

- have you been feeling symptoms of the postcollege blues? if so, what are they?

- how long have you been feeling like this?

- have your feelings been interfering with important aspects of your life (work, friends, family, romantic relationships)?

- what do you think triggered you to feel this way (be specific)?

- what have you done to cope with the postcollege blues?

- did these strategies make you feel better? why or why not?

powering up your positivity

Most of us, at some point in our lives, have met someone who seems to be happy all the time—where their natural state is simply one of consistent happiness. If something bad would happen to this person, such as getting into a terrible accident, developing cancer, or losing a loved one, they would of course suffer a great deal. But if you met up with them a short time later, you would see that they most likely would have returned to their original level of basic happiness. In contrast, take a person whose natural state seems to one of sadness and gloom and let something wonderful happen in their life, such as getting a good job, falling deeply in love, or coming into a great deal of money. This person would be happy for a while—but check back with them in a few weeks, months, or a year, and you will most likely find that this person has returned to their normal state of melancholy.

One major difference between these two types of people is their sense of life; that is, their general sense of how they perceive and experience the world. People who are generally happy process the events in their lives much differently than those whose natural disposition is one of unhappiness. Happy people hold brightly in the forefront of their consciousness the positive things in life while holding negative things in the background, whereas pessimists do the exact opposite. What this continues to show is that your own perceptions and attitudes about what you experience during your twenties have far more to do with your emotional state than any external events do.

what's your explanatory style?

No, this is not the latest pick-up line you will hear at a bar on a Saturday night. Your explanatory style is actually the way you describe the events that take place in your life. Seligman describes in his best-selling book *Learned Optimism: How to Change Your Mind and Your Life* that one of the most important factors in the development of learned helplessness is how you explain the events that happen in your life:

How you think about your problems, including depression itself, will either relieve depression or aggravate it. A failure or a defeat can teach you that you are now helpless, but learned helplessness will produce only momentary symptoms of depression—unless you have a pessimistic explanatory style. If you do, then failure and defeat can throw you into a full-blown depression. On the other hand, if your explanatory style is optimistic, your depression will be halted (1998, 75).

There are two major factors that determine your explanatory style. The first is what Seligman describes as *permanence*. This is when people perceive or explain negatives as permanent fixtures in their life. For example, a person with a pessimistic explanatory style believes that bad events are always going to happen, while someone with an optimistic explanatory style believes that bad events are only temporary and can be changed by their actions. The difference between the two is that a pessimist will think in permanent terms such as, "I will never find a job that I love," while an optimist will think in temporary terms such as, "The job I am in is not that great, but if I keep exploring I'll eventually find one I really enjoy." As Seligman explains, "If you think about bad things in terms of 'always' and 'never' and abiding traits, you have a permanent, pessimistic style. If you think in terms of 'sometimes' and 'lately' using qualifiers and blaming bad events on transient conditions, you have an optimistic style" (1998, 44).

But your explanatory style is not limited to how you view bad events. It also influences how you view the good experiences in your life. The interesting thing with this is that you use the opposite type of explaining when it comes to positive things. For example, people who are optimistic view positive events as permanent rather than temporary, and the opposite is true for pessimistic people, who believe that good events are temporary and fleeting. While optimists think in terms of, "I am good at what I do," pessimists will think, "I am just lucky." Seligman has found that:

> As for people who believe good events have permanent causes, when they succeed, they try even harder the next time. People who see temporary reasons for good events may give up even when they succeed, believing it was a fluke. People who best take advantage of success, and get on a role once things start going well, are the optimists (1998, 90).

The second component of your explanatory style is what Seligman describes as *pervasiveness*. As opposed to permanence, which determines how long a person feels helpless, pervasiveness determines whether the helplessness is limited to the original situation or is spread across many different situations. For example, say you lose your job because your company decided to outsource your position. Some people will restrict this negative event to the professional or financial aspect of their lives, while others will generalize the negativity that comes from the situation to all the areas of their life. An optimist will make specific explanations for their setbacks, while a pessimist will make more universal explanations. This is not to say that an optimistic person won't ever feel helpless when they lose their job—it's just that they will only feel like that for a little while and will eventually move forward. A pessimist, on the other hand, will let their whole life crumble to pieces because of one incident. And again, the opposite explanation effect holds true for good events. A pessimist will explain good events in terms of specific factors such as, "I got an A because I am smart in chemistry," while an optimist will explain good events in terms of universals such as, "I got an A because I am smart."

using your ABCDEs

One of the first steps you can take to develop this kind of optimism is learning to recognize and dispute pessimistic thoughts. If you learn to make permanent and universal explanations for good events, as well as temporary and specific explanations for bad events, you will begin developing your resilience against the postcollege blues and be able to bounce back when adversity hits. A simple but effective technique developed by Seligman in his book *Authentic Happiness: Using the New Positive Psychology to Realize Your Potential for Lasting Fulfillment* is the ABCDE technique (2004). **A** stands for adversity created by some event, **B** for pessimistic beliefs you have in response to the event, **C** for the usual consequences of your beliefs, **D** for you disputing the routine of your pessimistic beliefs, and **E** for the energy you create when you successfully dispute your pessimistic thoughts. Let's take a look at how this method can help you defeat your pessimistic thoughts.

Adversity: I have applied for job after job and have been unable to find work in my field.

Beliefs: No one wants to hire me. I will never find a job. I must not have very good qualifications. I am a total failure.

Consequences: I feel helpless and lost. I feel like I'm never going to find a job. I couldn't sleep last night. I have just wanted to be by myself all day and not talk to anyone.

Disputation: Maybe I'm just being unrealistic about this whole thing. The job market is not that good in my field. Maybe I need to start developing new skills or begin looking for jobs in other areas. I am not a total loser because I still think that I have a lot to offer a company. I just need to look and see what else is out there and keep trying.

Energizing: I am starting to feel better about myself now that I am looking at it from a more realistic perspective. I am now much more motivated to go looking for a new job. I am going to try to not let this type of negative thinking hold me back in the future.

Over the next week, find five situations in which some type of adversity comes up and, using your journal, explain them in terms of the example above. When doing this, pay special attention to your internal dialogue. If you begin hearing pessimistic thinking sneak in, dispute those thoughts using the ABCDEs. While you do this exercise, keep in mind that your beliefs are just that—*beliefs*—and you have the power to change them.

writing away the blues

When I asked twentysomethings about the strategies they use to make themselves feel better about something bad in their life, many said that they wrote down their thoughts and feelings in a journal. If you've never kept a journal or diary, chances are that you know someone who has. Most of the time people just write about daily events. However, a great deal of psychological research, shows that writing about how you feel is one of the best ways to cope with negative feelings.

Whenever you feel down about some part of your life, one of the first things you usually want to do is talk about what's troubling you. However, you may have difficulty expressing how you feel because you don't think people will understand, or you may be scared of what other people will think of you. As a result, you end up keeping your feelings locked up inside and never let anyone know what you're truly experiencing. It's easy to fall into the trap of trying to put up a front of being happy to save face in front of other twentysomethings. One of the major consequences of this saving-face phenomenon is that you may never have an opportunity to fully express how you are really feeling. These emotions gradually get buried deep inside, which blocks you from thinking about what you're experiencing in a broad and integrative way. By keeping your feelings bottled up, you struggle with a part of you that wants to express itself, creating a tug-of-war within your psyche that can make you even more stressed out.

Using a journal provides you with an outlet to express all that you're feeling and gives you an opportunity to better understand your experiences during your twenties. When you write down your thoughts and feelings, you start the process of coming face-to-face with the negative events in your life and begin confronting the thoughts and emotions you are feeling in response to those events. Using a journal gives you an opportunity to acknowledge what you are experiencing, which eventually forces you to rethink the events that have happened. This will help you understand your emotional response from a more realistic and rational perspective. When you write about experiences that you've been keeping inside, you will learn to translate those events into language. Once they are language based, you make them more concrete and can figure out ways to do something about the situation or how you are feeling. As Matthew McKay and Catharine Sutker describe in their book *The Self-Esteem Guided Journal*:

> Journaling offers a way to better understand and learn from your emotions, feelings, and thoughts. The process of putting words to paper elicits truths you may not even realize you possess. Writing gives you a certain distance and perspective, allowing you to better understand yourself. The ingrained patterns of self-perception become clear and visible on paper (2005, 3).

Expressing yourself through journal writing can also strengthen your vision of self by helping to improve your self-esteem through increasing your self-confidence. Expressive writing can help you master the way you experience negative events by increasing your ability to tolerate fear and reduce other negative emotions. As a result, your self-efficacy will increase because you begin to see yourself as having the ability to handle negative emotions effectively. When you're able to see yourself as having greater control over your emotional experiences, your negative moods will tend to dissipate much more quickly.

Believe it or not, expressive writing can also help you get a job! In an interesting study by psychologist Stefanie Spera and colleagues (1994) involving three groups of men who were recently laid off, one group was asked to write for thirty minutes a day for five consecutive days about their thoughts and feelings of being laid off. Another group was asked to write for the same period of time about how they were using their time while being unemployed, while the last group did not write at all and served as a comparison group. The researchers found that the men writing about their thoughts and feelings expressed the humiliation and outrage they felt about losing their jobs along with other intimate parts of their lives such as marital problems, illness, financial difficulties, and fears about the future. These men reported feeling better immediately after writing each day. At the end of three months, 23 percent of the men who wrote about their thoughts and feelings landed jobs compared with less than 5 percent of the men in the time management and no-writing comparison group. As the months progressed, 53 percent of those who wrote about their thoughts and feelings had jobs compared with only 18 percent of the men in the other conditions. What is particularly striking about the study was that the men in all three conditions had gone on the same number of job interviews. The only difference was that those who had written about their feelings were offered jobs.

Spera and her colleagues believe that the key to these findings was that those who had explored their thoughts and feelings were more likely to have come to terms with the anger and hostility they felt about their old job and toward their previous employer. Most of the men in the study had felt betrayed by their previous employers. Even during the initial interview for the study, the researchers often found it difficult to stop the men from venting their anger. The theory is that when most of them went on their job interviews, many tended to let down their guard and talked about how they were treated unfairly. Those who had written about their thoughts and feelings, on the other hand, were more likely to have come to terms with getting laid off, and during their interviews, these men came across as being less hostile and more promising employees.

beginning the process

Now, how should you go about the expressive writing process? In his book *Opening Up: The Healing Power of Expressing Emotions*, psychologist James W. Pennebaker, the leading researcher on journal therapy, suggests that it's not necessary to write about the most troubling things that have ever happened to you (1997). What seems to be more important is focusing on the issues that you're currently dealing with. Exploring both the objective experience (what happened) and your emotional response to it is what's key. You should feel that whenever there's something you want or need to express, you can always take a pen and paper out and just write it all down. When writing, make sure not to censor yourself in any way. You want to express everything that's going on in your head, just letting go and writing everything you feel. Also, it's not necessary to always write about negative things. Studies have found that focusing and writing about positive thoughts and feelings can have a similar therapeutic effect by acting as a buffer to the negative emotions you are feeling.

When you sit down to write, you will want to set aside about twenty to thirty minutes to allow enough time to explore your deepest thoughts and feelings. When actually writing, don't worry about grammar, spelling, or sentence structure. If you run out of things to say or reach a mental block, just repeat what you have already written and keep the process flowing. A former writing teacher of mine always emphasized the value of a good pen. I have found this extremely helpful in my journal writing because it allows my thoughts to just flow on to the paper without having to worry about pressing down hard to write.

Where and when you write will depend on your circumstances. Pennebaker suggests that the more unique the setting, the better. However, it's always good to find a place where you will not be interrupted or distracted by any sounds, sights, or smells. You may wonder if you need to write every day. Well, people seem to derive the same psychological benefits when writing simply when they feel like it. People with diaries often write every day, but most of those entries don't grapple with major psychological issues. What is important is the content, not the frequency. On the flip side, try not to write too much if you're using writing as a substitute for taking action or as some type of avoidance strategy.

A common question about fully expressing yourself on paper is what you should do with it after you're done. Pennebaker notes that anonymity is an important part of expressive writing. Many people will be inhibited and not fully express themselves if they think that others may read what they have written. Although this may be hard for you to do, I destroy most of what I write (unless I'll be using it for some future purpose). This allows me the opportunity to write whatever comes to my mind without worrying about anyone finding out what I am thinking or feeling. But do whatever you need to do to create a feeling of safety and anonymity.

Finally, while you can derive many benefits from expressive writing, it's not a panacea. What expressive writing can do is help you develop a better understanding of what you are experiencing during the turbulent twenties, which can then help you formulate a plan of action on how best to deal with what is troubling you. As McKay and Sutker explain:

Each day you'll learn how to notice positive qualities about yourself, begin taking on positive feedback others offer, and take note of evidence that points to your strengths and abilities. You'll develop a broader picture of yourself that includes a more accurate and healthy self-perception. You'll learn to avoid judging yourself so harshly (2005, 4).

Here are the steps to getting started with your writing process:

1. set aside twenty to thirty minutes in which you will not be disturbed.

2. focus on a difficult issue you are currently dealing with.

3. write about the objective experience—what actually happened—and your emotional response to it.

4. while you do this, don't censor yourself. express everything going on in your head. don't worry about grammar. just let it all flow out.

5. next, try to look at what you wrote and pick out the positive aspects of your situation. ask yourself what good can come out of the situation.

6. if you run out of things to say, keep repeating something positive until more things come to mind.

the exercise solution to depression

We all know that exercise can make you look and feel better, but were you aware that it is one of the most effective ways to fight anxiety and depression? Exercise's powerful psychological effects have been shown to consistently fight the blues and are even as effective as more traditional forms of treatment. In a study by psychiatrist John Griest and colleagues from the University of Wisconsin, two groups of patients with major depression were randomly assigned to either an exercise group that ran for forty minutes, three times a week, or to one of two forms of individual psychotherapy. At the end of ten weeks the participants in *all* three groups showed significant reductions in depression. What was significant was that there was no difference in improvement among the three groups. In other words, exercise worked just as well as psychotherapy. The researchers also found that the people who kept exercising continued to show improvement at the one, three, six, and nine-month follow-ups (1979).

Antidepressant medication is currently the number-one form of therapy for depression and yet even though more and more antidepressants are being recommended each year, the rate of depression continues to increase and shows no signs of slowing down. More importantly, antidepressants can be expensive and carry unwanted side effects such as dizziness, dry mouth, nausea, and sexual dysfunction. So how does exercise compare? In a sixteen-week study by James Blumenthal and colleagues at Duke University, participants were assigned to an exercise group, an antidepressant group, or a combination group. The exercise group exercised for thirty minutes, three times a week, while the medication group received the popular antidepressant Zoloft, and subjects in the exercise/medication group received the same type of medication and performed the same exercise regimen as those in the two other groups. At the end of sixteen weeks the researchers found that *all three* groups experienced reductions in depressive symptoms. Over 60 percent of those in the exercise group no longer met the diagnostic criteria for major depressive disorder, compared to 68 percent of the people in the medication group, and 65 percent of those in the exercise/medication group. In other words, exercise alone was comparable to the effectiveness of antidepressant medication and comparable to medication combined with exercise in alleviating the subjects' symptoms of depression (1999).

Michael Babyak and his colleagues at Duke then followed these people for six months after the initial study and found that the subjects who continued to exercise were much less likely to see their depression return than the individuals who relied on medication alone or used a combination of both medication and exercise. In fact, only 8 percent of those in the exercise group relapsed, compared to 38 percent of those in the medication group, and 31 percent of those in the medication/exercise group (2000). This means that over four times as many people relapsed when they used antidepressants compared to people who used exercise alone!

how soon will you begin feeling better?

One question you may have is how quickly you will start feeling better after beginning to exercise regularly. Well, this answer depends on a number of factors. Individual characteristics and the seriousness of a person's emotional state must always be taken into account. However, Dr. Fernando Dimeo and his colleagues have found that you can start deriving the mood-elevating benefits of exercise right from your first workout (2001). Dimeo took twelve people diagnosed with moderate to severe depression and had them exercise on a treadmill for thirty minutes a day for ten days. Dimeo found that their symptoms had dropped by an average of 33 percent. In fact, five of the patients had their depression scores decrease by over 50 percent in only ten days. What is even more surprising is that exercise worked faster than antidepressant drugs, which generally take two to four weeks to begin working.

which exercise is best?

Is there a specific type of exercise that is best for relieving depression? The research has found that the most effective form of exercise is the one you like the most, because consistency seems to be the most important factor in producing mood-elevating effects. Walking, running, swimming, aerobic dance, weight training, and yoga have all been shown to produce similar antidepressant effects. Whatever exercise you use, you will want to do it at least three times a week for about twenty-five to thirty minutes. You also don't have to exercise at a high intensity to get the mental health benefits described above. Again, consistency is what matters most.

creating your own exercise prescription

When developing your own program, you will want to keep the following in mind to get the most out of exercising.

Do something you enjoy. While I was a personal trainer I found this to be one of the most important things to consider when starting an exercise program. If you're not having fun while you are exercising, not only will you be spending your time in a bad experience, but you will most likely lose motivation pretty quickly and not stick to your program. One thing to look at when thinking about the kind of exercise you like is whether you like exercising by yourself or in a group. Quite often, group activities like exercise classes, walking in a group, or organized sports are great ways to get exercise that also add a social component, which can increase your enjoyment and adherence. So answer the following questions:

- what kind of exercise do you like?

- why do you like it?

- do you like doing it by yourself or in a group?

- do you enjoy exercising inside, outdoors, or both?

Get specific. When thinking about your program, you will want to get specific about what you want to accomplish. To help you with your goals, apply the goal-setting techniques you learned about in chapter 2 to your exercise program. Try to set both long- and short-term goals, figure out what you need to do to accomplish them, and then in your journal measure your progress (both physical and mental).

Keep it realistic. One thing you want to keep in mind when making your goals is keeping them realistic. If you set your goals too high or think you're suddenly going to start exercising five times a week for two hours a day, you may be setting yourself up for failure. This kind of common error can actually increase your sense of helplessness because it seems like you can't even control this aspect of your life. So start out with a realistic goal—somthing like exercising three times a week for twenty to thirty minutes. As you integrate physical activity in your life, you can gradually increase the intensity or frequency.

trying out therapy

Some twentysomethings I spoke to said that one of the paths they took to deal with the struggles they were having with the postcollege blues was seeking out professional help. They told me that seeing a psychologist gave them an opportunity to fully express to an outside observer what they were truly feeling and it really helped them get through many of the issues they were dealing with at the time. "I decided to start seeing a therapist about a year after I graduated," says Michael, a twenty-four-year-old from Baltimore. "I was pretty darn lonely and didn't really feel like I had a group of friends whom I trusted. I really missed my family as well as my close friends who were back east. I started seeing a psychiatrist for about six months, but I didn't feel like I was making much progress so I really shopped around and saw about five psychotherapists before settling down with a new one whom I have been seeing since. I'm glad I went because I think it helps a lot. I have found that it's really useful just to take an hour a week to think about yourself. I still have a lot of issues to work out and I think therapy is a great way to figure out those things."

As Michael points out, therapy can provide an opportunity to take a step back and evaluate important issues that need to be addressed in your life. Not only will you be able to have an objective person listen to everything you are going through, but a good therapist will also help you develop the psychological skills needed to cope with many of the issues you will confront during the turbulent twenties.

letting go of the fear of appearing weak

One of the obstacles that young people can face in seeing a psychologist is that they can feel weak for having to see a professional to deal with their postcollege blues. The idea that it's not normal for someone in their early twenties to seek out therapy can prevent many twentysomethings from getting much-needed help. Most twentysomethings don't have friends or know people their own age seeing a psychologist. Even if there are such people around, you may not be aware of it because no one really wants to mention that they're seeking professional help because of the stigma usually attached to it. "Back when I started therapy, I really didn't have friends who were seeing therapists, so it was a tough step," says Gabriel, a twenty-six-year-old from Albuquerque. "I talked to my parents about it and then spent some time looking at therapists covered by my insurance. I do think the stigma of therapy really goes away when you have a lot of friends who are also in therapy. My two best guy friends are in therapy, the two girls I've dated seriously both see therapists, and various other folks are in therapy, too. In fact, at least three of my friends are open about the fact that they also see psychiatrists so they can get antidepressants. Many of those who are not in therapy wish they had insurance programs that covered it. I still don't really mention it at work, but I'm pretty open with all my friends about seeing a therapist, and I find myself constantly recommending therapy to those of my friends who aren't already in it. I do think that I'd feel much less comfortable talking about therapy if there weren't so many folks around me who also see therapists." As Gabriel points out, unless you know of people who are actually in therapy, it can be tough to let go of the fear and seek out professional help.

I asked psychologist Lynn Bufka, a director in the Practice department at the American Psychological Association, about this and she told me:

> I think more people might consider therapy if they under-stood it and knew that therapy doesn't have to go on for years, but can be brief and focused on problem-solving. This is why a therapist might offer something more than a good friend can. As a practitioner, I really think people would be better served if they thought of psychotherapy as something that you might avail yourself of at a particular juncture in your life rather than having to see a therapist for years. We see our physicians that way—why not treat mental health the same way? (June 9, 2005)

Bufka makes a great point: If you were seriously hurt physically, you would certainly take the necessary steps to treat your injury. Well, if your emotions or way of thinking have been seriously injured, it is also necessary to take the proper steps to treat your pain, and some-times this means seeking out professional help. As a good friend of mine who went to see a therapist told me, "I really just figured it came down to wanting to take some steps to feel better and thinking that this might be a good way to do it. If I were physically sick I would probably spend the money to get that treated, so I figured I would just try to eat out fewer times over the next few months and not go out as much."

shopping for a psychologist

In looking for a good psychologist, Bufka told me, "I think it's really important for people to feel comfortable selecting and hiring. I mean, it is hiring—the patient is the one paying for the services of a therapist," and because you can pay a significant amount of money to see a professional, it is a good idea to shop for a psychologist like you would anything else you're buying. Here are some helpful tips she said to keep in mind when seeking a psychologist:

1. **Call potential therapists and ask questions.** Don't just go on whether or not they have an available opening. You're signing up for something pretty personal, so feeling comfortable with the psychologist, whether it is inter-personal comfort or comfort with how they respond to your initial questions, does matter. You are the pur-chaser of services, so ask questions. If you don't like the answers, don't make an appointment.

2. **Inquire about fees and whether they will accept your insurance up front.** Don't leave any doubt that you could see the person if you like them. Also, ask whether the therapist has a sliding scale. Many therapists feel a responsibility to treat a certain number of lower-income clients, and this may make it possible to see someone who is out of your price range.

3. Provide a little bit of information about your current situation and see if the psychologist seems responsive. This may be an indication of how they will be during therapy.

4. Either on the phone or in person, ask questions about how long the therapist thinks treatment might take. Ask about their approach to therapy and what you might be doing. Most experienced therapists can be rather eclectic in approach. This is generally a good thing because it means they are paying attention to the literature, striving to learn new things, and adapting to meet the needs of the person in front of them.

there really are no such things as problems

In reading this header you may be saying to yourself, "Well, I have some serious problems in *my* life." But if you took a step back and looked at your problems from a realistic and optimistic perspective, with very few exceptions where things are completely beyond your control, you would see that many of the things you think of as problems are simply points where a decision has to be made. For example, if your job is making you miserable, you have the decision to either stick it out or find a new one. If you're feeling lonely, you can choose to sit at home and continue to think that no one likes you or you can be proactive and go out and develop new friendships. If you're struggling financially, you can continue to worry and stress out about it or you can learn new skills to get a higher-paying job and/or learn how to save and invest your money more wisely. If a valuable relationship is deteriorating, you can choose to let it get worse or you can make the decision to understand the situation better and work harder to mend it. The problems that are causing you so much distress and sadness during your twenties will fade once you make the decision to act and do something about the situation. If your postcollege blues are starting to interfere with important areas of your life, you can make the decision to go see a therapist. The choice to be proactive and change your life is usually the harder path to take and that is exactly why so few people follow it. However, when you do take responsibility for how you want to feel, you will begin conquering the postcollege blues and provide yourself with opportunities for happiness and fulfillment.

books you will love

Learned Optimism: How to Change Your Mind and Your Life (1998) and *Authentic Happiness: Using the New Positive Psychology to Realize Your Potential for Lasting Fulfillment* (2004) by **Martin Seligman.** The author created a major shift in the psychological community with the idea that psychology had to start focusing on how to create happiness instead of just focusing on mental illness. Seligman, the founder of positive psychology, integrates decades of psychology research into a practical guide on how to develop an optimistic sense of life.

Opening Up: The Healing Power of Expressing Emotions (1997) by **James Pennebaker.** A great resource for getting the most out of your journal writing.

The Self-Esteem Guided Journal (2005) by **Matthew McKay** and **Catharine Sutker.** An excellent psychological workbook on how to use guided journaling to increase your self-esteem. The book provides numerous techniques on how to use expressive writing to silence the pathological critic.

chapter 5

how do you survive in today's working world?

Work saves us from three great evils: boredom, vice, and need.—Voltaire

"The gut-wrenching question that kept entering my head several months after graduation was, 'I went through sixteen-plus years of education and thirty thousand dollars of debt for this?'" says Jamie, a twenty-five-year old from San Francisco. "In school I wasn't given an accurate account of what to expect as an entry-level professional. I was told by my nurturing professors and cheerful career services counselors that I could go anywhere and do anything with my Notre Dame degree. I knew nothing about being a 'bottom dweller,' the 'coffee wench,' or 'putting in my dues' as I have painfully come to know now so well."

For most twentysomethings, the first order of business after college is looking for a new job. However, what graduates quickly discover upon entering today's working world is that finding a job, especially one that is fulfilling, is not as easy as they assumed it would be. This can come as quite a shock because, as Jamie points out, twentysomethings assume that after spending so much time and money getting a college education, it should be a snap to get a good job. But ask any twentysomething about their work experiences since graduation and they will tell you that it has actually been one of the most stressful as well as disappointing aspects of their postcollege lives.

Dr. Mel Levine, a pediatric professor at the University of North Carolina Medical School, believes that part of the reason why graduates are having such a hard time entering the working world is because they emerge from college with an unrealistic picture of the world. He blames overprotective parents and coddling colleges who lavish students with praise and tell them that once they get their education, they can be anything they want. In a recent Associated Press article Levine says, "We're seeing an epidemic of people who are having a hard time making the transition to work—kids who had too much success early in life and who have become accustomed to instant gratification" (Irvine 2005). I spoke to Barry Schwartz about this situation and he told me, "The problem is that we try to give our students a sense that anything is possible. We think we are doing them a favor, but we are actually making their lives more stressful. Maybe it worked at other points in history, but not for this generation."

Twentysomethings I spoke to told me that while all the praise and hype that parents and colleges give them can be a positive motivator for working hard during school, the downside is that it paints an unrealistic picture of the working world and provides no real help in dealing with what they actually experience at work during their twenties. Some of the biggest complaints I've heard from twentysomethings is that no one ever really informed them of the real challenges and hazards they would face in today's job market; no one told them about the possibility of having to look for six or more months to find a job in what they majored in; no one said that their job wasn't going to be as interesting and stimulating as what they experienced during class; no one lets them know that much of what they learned academically would have little or no value in the work they actually do; and certainly no one mentioned that they would not be able to work in whatever job their heart desired.

In addition to this unrealistic picture, twentysomethings are coming out of college without many of the skills needed to adapt and thrive in the new economy that has emerged at the beginning of the twenty-first century. In many ways, our educational system has not kept up with the dramatic changes that have taken place over the past few decades. The new economic reality is that to succeed in today's marketplace, you need much more than a high IQ or good analytical and reasoning abilities. What is becoming essential in today's global working world are skills that are less academic and much more psychological in nature. Aptitudes such as self-awareness, emotional regulation, resilience, initiative, optimism, adaptability, empathy, relationship building, and persuasiveness are now needed at every level of business. And as Daniel Goleman has found:

... for children of the meritocracy, who were taught that education and technical skills were a permanent ticket to success—this new way of thinking may come as a shock. People are beginning to realize that success takes more than intellectual excellence or technical prowess, and that we need another sort of skill just to survive—and certainly to thrive—in the increasingly turbulent job market (1998, 11).

Parents and our educational system assume that you will pick up these psychological intelligence skills somewhere along the way. Maybe in the past this was adequate, but it is becoming less of a viable option today. As the marketplace continues to rapidly change, so do the skills that are needed to succeed. Therefore, the purpose of this chapter is not only to explain why these skills are shaping the nature of work but also to show you how to build the foundation for developing them so that you can begin thriving in today's working world.

the creation of a brave new working world

"I think people our age are living much different lives than past generations," says Ben, a twenty-five-year-old from Boston. "My parents went to college, worked in stable jobs, and were married by the time they were my age, but it's not like that at all for me or my friends. Today, there are so many paths to choose from, you only stay with a job for a couple of years, and it's very likely that your job will take you to the other side of the country away from your family and friends. It can be pretty rough out there because there are so many other people trying to compete for the same opportunities you are. I have tons of friends who cannot find good jobs and are working at bars and cafés. It just seems like life is so much more intense today. Sometimes all the opportunities can seem great, but other times the instability of it all can be really stressful and overwhelming."

What Ben is articulately describing are some of the major differences between the working world our parents experienced during their twenties and the one today's graduates are transitioning into after college. In a very short period of time, the world economy has transformed from one built on manufacturing to one built on information. Muscle-work is rapidly being replaced by mind-work and in the process has created a global economy that revolves around scientific and technological breakthroughs, constant change, and an unparalleled level of competitiveness. Advancement in computers is helping research-and-development laboratories come out with technological discoveries at an unprecedented rate, with the discovery of new knowledge, products, and services coming out on almost a daily basis. The Internet has made it possible for virtually anyone to enter the marketplace, and this advancement in technology combined with the adoption of free-market ideals around the globe is allowing millions of people to enter the world economy.

Today, money moves faster than ever. Ideas that are hot and capture the imagination one moment are quickly replaced by newer and better ideas. Businesses are quickly created, they grow rapidly and thrive, and then are gone in a blink of an eye. Along with businesses popping in and out of existence, so do many jobs. Although this creative destruction has resulted in a consistent explosion of new information and technology as well as new products and services, it has led to an extremely volatile job market. It was only a generation ago that you could find stable employment after college that promised a relatively comfortable standard of living. This is no longer the case in the twenty-first century, and as Goleman explains:

> It seems no one is guaranteed a job *anywhere* anymore. These are troubled times for workers. The creeping sense that no one's job is safe, even as the companies they work for are thriving, means the spread of fear, apprehension, and confusion (1998, 10).

All of these changes have resulted in twentysomethings transitioning into the most competitive marketplace in history.

the three As that are changing the nature of work

No, these As aren't letter grades you got in three of your classes in college. They are what Daniel Pink describes in his book *A Whole New Mind: Moving from the Information Age to the Conceptual Age* as the three major forces that are changing the very nature of the work available to today's college graduates. As Pink explains, "We are moving from an economy and a society built on the logical, linear, computer-like capabilities of the Information Age to an economy and society built on inventive, empathetic, big-picture capabilities of what's rising in its place, the Conceptual Age," and the three forces that are driving this change are *abundance*, *Asia*, and *automation* (2005, 1).

the price of abundance

The first of the forces Pink describes, abundance, deals with the extraordinary increase in just about everything that has been created by the rise of the information age. This abundance has enhanced our lives by providing us with low-cost, high-quality goods and services. However, it has also created an ironic by-product that is dramatically changing the working world twentysomethings are entering into after college graduation: the very skills that produced this overabundance are also becoming less important in the marketplace. Because of the basic economic principle of supply and demand, the more there is of any one product, the less it is desired. But not only is the product less desired because there is so much of it, but so are the skills that were used to create that product. As a result, today's world of overabundance is causing the logic and analytic reasoning skills that created the information age to become less valued in the economy of the twenty-first century.

the path of least resistance

The second force, Asia, is impacting the working lives of today's twentysomethings by acquiring many of the jobs that were once the bread and butter of recent graduates. The reason why we're seeing so many jobs that twentysomethings would typically work in after graduation move overseas is simply because young people in Asia can do things cheaper than their counterparts in the Western world. Think about it: why would you pay an American who recently graduated with a degree in computer science sixty thousand dollars a year to do programming when you can have someone in India do it for twelve thousand dollars?

But not only is it cheaper to outsource this kind of knowledge work—it is also much more efficient. As Thomas Friedman, *New York Times* columnist and author of *The World Is Flat: A Brief History of the Twenty-first Century*, explains, "The second dirty little secret, which several prominent American CEOs told me only in a whisper, goes like this: When they send jobs abroad, they not only save 75 percent on wages, they get a 100 percent increase in productivity" (2005b, 260). Rajesh Rao, a young Indian entrepreneur who started an electronic-gaming company in Bangalore, told Friedman:

> There is no time to rest. That it is gone. There are dozens of people who are doing the same thing you are doing, and they are trying to do it better. It is like water in a tray; you shake it, and it will find the path of least resistance. That is what is going to happen to so many jobs—they will go to that corner of the world where there is the least resistance and the most opportunity (2005b, 190).

It is this path of least resistance that is turning today's working world into the most competitive in history, and if our schools continue to educate students in skills that can easily be outsourced to young people who can do it cheaper and better, then many twentysomethings here are going to find themselves without a job and living at home with mom and dad. This message is being echoed throughout the business world by entrepreneurs such as Bill Gates. In a speech to our nation's governors, Gates explained to them:

> America's high schools are obsolete ... By obsolete, I mean that our high schools—even when they're working exactly as designed—cannot teach our kids what they need to know

today. Training the workforce of tomorrow with the high schools of today is like trying to teach kids about today's computers on a fifty-year-old mainframe. It's the wrong tool for the times. Our high schools were designed fifty years ago to meet the needs of another age. Until we design them to meet the needs of the twenty-first century, we will keep limiting—even ruining—the lives of millions of Americans every year (2005).

TurboTax rules!

Did you use TurboTax to do your taxes this year? Well, if you did, then you are contributing to the third factor that is changing the future of work. This force has to do with the continued evolution of machines that make our lives more convenient. As computers and technology become more advanced, it becomes easier for jobs that can be reduced to a set of rules or broken down into a set of repeatable steps to either be outsourced to Asia or automated by machines. Back when I graduated in 2000, almost anybody with decent computer skills could get a job as a programmer. This isn't the case anymore as an increasing number of routine-type jobs are being done by more efficient and cost-effective automated methods. The embodiment of this automation comes from Appligenics, a British company that has created software that can write software. Typically, a human being can write about four hundred lines of computer code a day. Guess how fast Appligenics can write the code: *four hundred lines in less than a second!* As Daniel Pink explains, "If a five hundred dollar-a-month Indian charted accountant doesn't swipe your comfortable accounting job, TurboTax will" (2005, 14).

we are entitled to nothing

"My first year after college I spent in a foreign country," says twenty-five-year-old Maria. "This was a nice time but not exactly the real world. My life was pretty much like it was in college, without the pressure of grades. When I finally got back to America, the economy was in bad shape and it was impossible to find a job. I actually had to look for a whole year and a half before finding my current job. I am now working as an administrative assistant and I really hate it. It's very hard going from such a strong academic background, where you are used to being on top, to feeling like a loser because you can't find a job. I was very depressed and antisocial for a long time. Because I went to a really competitive school and worked so hard during college, I was led to believe that I deserved to find a good job (my dream job) quickly. It is really disappointing that I did not end up where I wanted right away, even though I finally found a job. But I'm hoping this will only be very temporary."

A few years ago, a good friend of mine told me, "I don't know why I can't get a job. I have a college degree." During our senior year, he really didn't make too much of an effort to search for jobs because he assumed that there would be plenty offered to him. But as his unemployment stretched into many months after graduation, he slowly started to realize that something wasn't right. It wasn't until he worked for a few years in low-level jobs that it finally began to sink in that just because you have a college degree doesn't mean that you are entitled to a good job.

Because of the Three As, a college education entitles you to nothing anymore. White-collar jobs that most college graduates look forward to during their twenties are either being shipped overseas or are being eliminated altogether by machines and automation. In a conversation with the consular official who oversees the granting of visas at the U.S. Embassy in Beijing about the economic and social changes that are taking place around the world, Thomas Friedman was told:

> I do think Americans are oblivious to the huge changes. Every American who comes over to visit me [in China] is just blown away ... Your average kid in the U.S. is growing up in a wealthy country with many opportunities, and many are the kids of advantaged, educated people who have a sense of entitlement. Well, the hard reality for that kid is that fifteen years from now Wu is going to be his boss and Zhou is going to be the doctor in town. The competition is coming, and many of the kids are going to move into their twenties clueless about the rising forces (2005b, 264).

a new kind of work intelligence

Aside from grades, the most common way we measure intelligence is through standardized tests. We have the PSAT, SAT, GRE, GMAT, LSAT, MCAT. Each one of these tests measures two basic ways of thinking: logic and analysis. Daniel Pink (2005) calls this a "SAT-ocracy" and if you are someone who is good at taking tests and using linear, sequential reasoning in a short period of time, then you will probably do quite well on these exams (and have a high IQ).

The focus on this type of intelligence certainly has had its advantages. As Pink describes, it has released people from the stranglehold of aristocratic privilege and opened up educational and professional opportunities to a diverse set of people. It has also propelled the world economy and lifted the living standards of millions. But because of the Three As, a growing amount of psychological research is showing that the logic and analytical testing system that has been the gatekeeper to middle-class society has a major flaw: it is not testing for the psychological skills that are becoming essential in today's working world. And because they are not being tested for, they are not being taught to students.

What psychologists like Daniel Goleman have found is that high academic intelligence is beginning to take a back seat to other types of intelligence in determining success in the working world. As Goleman has discovered during his intelligence research:

> Given how much emphasis schools and admissions put on it, IQ alone explains surprisingly little of achievement at work or in life. When IQ test scores are correlated with how well people perform in their careers, the highest estimate of how much difference IQ accounts for is about 25 percent. A careful analysis, though, suggests a more accurate figure may be no higher than 10 percent, and perhaps as low as 4 percent (1998, 19).

What this means is that about 75 to 90 percent of your success in the working world is not associated with your IQ and is the result of something else: your psychological intelligence.

So far you have learned ways to increase your psychological intelligence to help you figure out who you are, who you want to become, and how to conquer the postcollege blues. Now we're going to focus on the areas of psychological intelligence that you can apply to your work life to help you become a better employee, adapt to change, and create happiness in any type of job you're in. The psychological intelligence skills that will help you do this are emotional intelligence, cultural intelligence, and flow.

bringing emotional intelligence to your work

While writing this book, I was taking classes for my master's degree in organizational management. As I was working on this chapter, I took a class on negotiation and conflict management, and during one of my classes our professor had us do a mock negotiation of three people trying to settle a dispute within an organization. Two other classmates and I were each given a role and asked to act out the personalities of each of the employees. I was a software developer in charge of developing a new missile defense software program for the government. The setup for the negotiation was that there had been bad blood between me and the contract manager, and because we had been unable to work well together, a situation had arisen where the project's completion could possibly be late—with a fine of ten thousand dollars for each day it was delayed. The role of the project manager was to bring the contract manager and myself together to come up with a solution to the problem.

So we proceeded to act out our parts and got into some heated arguments during the negotiation. Each of us tried to communicate our positions effectively, made an effort to persuade each other about where we were coming from, and tried to convince the project manager to take our side. But because tempers flared (because this was part of our role), we went around in circles and most of the time talked at each other instead of with each other. The project manager, on the other hand, was trying to keep the peace by preventing the two of us from letting the meeting turn into a shouting match. What the project manager was trying to create was an environment in which the contract manager and I could openly discuss the dilemma, listen to each other's perspectives, and come up with a solution to the problematic situation. If the project manager could not effectively communicate her message and manage the conflict in a way that facilitated all parties agreeing on a solution, then the project would fail.

In thinking about the situation above, ask yourself what skills were needed to come to a productive solution. Each party had to manage their emotions so that they did not interfere with effectively communicating their message. They had to recognize what the other person was saying, why they were saying it, and make arguments against these points in order to persuade the other party to see things from their perspective. And in the end, if they were unable to get along, then either they would not negotiate an agreement or they would come to a solution that some or all of the parties didn't like, creating bad relationships that could negatively affect the organization for years to come. After we were done with the mock negotiation, my professor, Mike Stouder, explained to us that these kinds of situations arise everyday in an organization and told us, "In the past, people used to work with knowledge and materials. Today we are working with people, and the ability to manage relationships and conflict is vitally important. Today, we're getting more done by informal networks of relationships, and if you don't know how to build them, then you're not going to do well in the organization."

academic intelligence will only take you so far

Stouder's description of how the nature of work is changing gives us a clue about how psychological skills are becoming the backbone of success in today's global economy. In a world with an overabundance of knowledge, we are having to work with a variety of people to get things done because other people have the kind of knowledge we need to accomplish our goals. As the sheer quantity of information continues to mount, two things happen. First, since we cannot know everything about everything, we have to begin focusing our attention on a specific area within our field. As even more information becomes available, we have to continue specializing just to keep up. However, as we do this, sooner or later we can become out of touch with certain areas within our field. As a result, if you need to get a large or complicated project done, you will need access to the knowledge you don't have. You do this by working across those informal networks Stouder was talking about. Because other people will have specialized knowledge that you need, you will have to build and manage relationships with those people so that you can negotiate a situation that provides mutual benefit for both parties.

Secondly, within your specialized area, everyone has access to the same information. More and more people are getting higher levels of education, so what now sets you apart is not how much you know but rather how you can effectively communicate your knowledge when working with others to get something accomplished. As Lyle Spencer Jr., director of research and technology at Hay/McBer Consulting, told Goleman about the role of academic knowledge today:

> What you learned in school distinguishes superior performers in only a handful of the five or six hundred jobs for

which we've done competence studies. It's just a threshold competence; you need it to get into the field, but it does not make you a star. It's the emotional intelligence abilities that matter more for superior performance (1998, 19).

In fact, what Goleman has found is that compared to expertise and IQ, emotional competence is worth *twice* as much when it comes to performing successfully in a job. He also found that on average, close to 90 percent of successful leadership within organizations is attributable to emotional intelligence.

Now, this is not to say that technical knowledge doesn't have a place in today's working world. It pays to have expertise in the area you're working in, but because of the Three As and the world of overabundance, psychological intelligence is becoming more and more relevant in today's rapidly changing, highly precarious, diverse, global working world. As Goleman explains, "In the new workplace, with its emphasis on flexibility, teams, and a strong customer orientation, this crucial set of emotional competencies is becoming increasingly essential for excellence in every job and in every part of the world" (1998, 29), and it is important that twentysomethings understand that this is becoming the new standard for the jobs that are available after graduation.

using emotional intelligence at your job

I touched upon emotional intelligence in chapter 3 when I discussed how important it is to be aware of your emotions in making good decisions. But to see how emotional intelligence impacts your work life, we need a much more detailed description of what it is. Goleman defines *emotional intelligence* as:

... the capacity for recognizing our own feelings, and those of others, for motivating ourselves, and for managing our emotions well in ourselves and in our relationships. It describes abilities distinct from, but complementary to, academic intelligence, the purely cognitive capacities measured by IQ. Many people who are book smart but lack emotional intelligence end up working for people who have lower IQs than they but who excel in emotional intelligence skills (1998, 317).

Emotional intelligence is made up of five psychological intelligence skills: self-awareness, self-regulation, motivation, empathy, and social skills. Let's take a look at how each builds upon another.

self-awareness and emotional regulation

The foundation for building your emotional intelligence begins with paying greater attention to what you are feeling in the moment and using your inner signals as a guide in responding to the situations you face at work. When you increase your awareness of your emotions, you can use this knowledge to keep disruptive emotions and impulses in check so that they do not interfere with the tasks you're trying to accomplish. For example, if a task or work relationship is stressing you out and you're not aware of it, your emotions can run amok and negatively affect your performance. The more accurately you can sense your emotions and how they are shaping your view of a work situation, the better able you'll be at fine-tuning your actions so you can deal with the stressful situation in a productive manner.

Being highly self-aware will also give you a more accurate assessment of what your strengths and weaknesses are at work. If you're unaware of what you are capable of in your job, then you may put yourself in situations that are overwhelming and will cause you a great deal of stress and anxiety. By knowing what you're capable of, you will be secure in your self-efficacy and only put yourself in situations where you know that your skills will not be overstretched.

performing with grace under pressure

In high school, my humanities teacher, Ken Jenkins, had us read *The Old Man and the Sea* by Ernest Hemmingway. In the novel, the narrator talks about Joe DiMaggio, the former baseball player for the New York Yankees. DiMaggio was one of Mr. Jenkins' favorite players, and he seemed to bring him up in almost every single class. He loved DiMaggio so much because Mr. Jenkins admired him for playing so many years with a severe injury to his foot. DiMaggio had a bone spur, an extremely painful condition that is often debilitating, but he loved the game so much that he managed his pain and did not let it affect his motivation to become the greatest baseball player he could be. Mr. Jenkins would always tell us that DiMaggio was an example of performing with grace under pressure, and it's this ability to stay motivated in the face of challenges and setbacks that is one of the most important emotional intelligence skills that you can develop.

Motivating yourself and staying positive when the going gets tough rests on the first two components of your emotional intelligence. As you saw in chapter 3, you use your emotions to move and guide you in the direction you want to go in life. By being aware of your emotions and learning to regulate them, you can eventually harness their power to help you take action and achieve your goals. In addition, by using the positive psychology techniques you learned in chapter 4, you can create an optimistic view of life and fend off anxiety that can come from stressful or painful situations.

One aspect of motivation that is becoming an important skill to have in today's marketplace is your ability to adapt in the face of constant change. The economy has vastly changed in the last ten years, and the ability to adjust to a rapidly changing working world by regulating your emotions and staying motivated in the midst of obstacles and ambiguity will give you a competitive advantage over others in your field.

people skills

Emotional awareness and self-regulation are also the foundation for the final two aspects of emotional intelligence: empathy and social skills. Today, you have to work with an array of people from a variety of different backgrounds to get your goals accomplished. This is now the norm in today's global economy, and if you are unable to build relationships with those people and gather their expertise, it will be difficult to create and innovate. One of the major factors in building good relationships is both sensing what others are feeling and being able to see things from their perspective. This is the essence of being an empathetic person. By making an effort to better understand what other people are feeling, you will start building relationships with a broad diversity of people based on the universality of human emotions.

Being able to read other people adds to your overall communication skills, because when you understand where your coworkers are coming from, you will be better able to fine-tune your response based on what they feel about the present work situation. This ability to communicate has far-reaching effects on your work life because the ability to send clear and convincing messages is essential for social skills such as persuading others to see your point of view, negotiating and resolving disagreements, or leading coworkers by inspiring and guiding them.

increasing your emotional intelligence

Unlike IQ, which does not change much as we grow older, emotional intelligence continues to develop as you learn and grow from your experiences in life. In studies that have tracked people's level of emotional intelligence, Goleman has found that "... people get better and better in these capabilities as they grow more adept at handling their own emotions and impulses, at motivating themselves and at honing their empathy and social adroitness. There is an old-fashioned word for this growth in emotional intelligence: *maturity*" (1998, 7).

One thing you should keep in mind is that increasing your emotional intelligence (or any other aspect of your psychological intelligence) does not quite work like increasing your academic intelligence. You can say, "I am going to learn about the civil war," then go read a book and the day after recall the knowledge you just learned. But you can't say, "I am going to have high emotional intelligence," and then the next day suddenly be able to recognize emotions in others or be a great leader who can persuade and motivate others. The truth is, increasing your emotional intelligence is a gradual process because it takes time to keep these skills in your conscious awareness within the context of what you are trying to do at work, and then more time to integrate them into your subconscious so that they become an automatic way of thinking.

A good way to view this psychological process is by thinking about how you learned to drive a car. When you first began driving, you had to constantly remind yourself of all the things you needed to do at each moment. While driving, you were consciously thinking, "Okay, press the gas pedal slightly, let go of the clutch a little, keep your hands on the steering wheel, get ready to shift gears, look around to see that no one is coming," along with a multitude of other thoughts. But today, you drive down the street without thinking about it, as if it were second nature. This is because the skills you learned have become integrated into your subconscious by driving a lot and practicing your skills. These memories help guide you when you drive and can be retrieved instantaneously from past experiences so that you can react to a variety of situations. Well, the same learning process takes place when you try to increase your emotional intelligence.

For example, say you are trying to increase your emotional awareness and ability to regulate what you are feeling. In a stressful situation at work, first you may have to consciously think, "Okay, what exactly am I feeling right now? Do I need to take a step back and see if what I'm feeling is appropriate to the situation? I don't want to let what is happening carry me away. I'll look for more facts and check to see if my emotions are appropriate." In another social situation, you may need to be empathetic toward a coworker. Now you may be thinking, "Pay attention to what their expression is. What are they feeling? Try to see things from their perspective. How can I make them feel better?" At first, you will have to keep these kind of thoughts in your conscious awareness; but as you continue to practice, just like you did with driving a car, this way of thinking will become integrated into your subconscious and be automatic when dealing with future social situations.

emotional intelligence checklist

You can practice integrating this new way of thinking by using the following questions in situations that call upon your emotional intelligence skills.

self-awareness

☐ am I paying attention to exactly what I am feeling (for instance, anger, sadness, frustration) in stressful situations?

☐ am I exploring why i'm responding in such a manner?

☐ am I trying to make a connection between what I'm thinking and what i'm feeling?

☐ am I staying aware of what directions my emotions are leading me and why?

☐ am I taking note of how my emotions are affecting my performance?

self-regulation

☐ when I encounter a stressful situation, am I taking a step back and assessing whether my emotions are appropriate to the situation?

☐ am I taking a time-out to clear my mind and focus my energy when negative emotions surface?

☐ am I preventing distressing feelings from taking over my mind and ability to concentrate at work?

motivation

- [ ] am I striving to improve and get better at what I am doing?

- [ ] am I setting realistic challenges and goals?

- [ ] am I putting myself in a situation where I get constant feedback?

- [ ] am I ready to seize opportunities?

- [ ] am I persisting in my goals in the face of obstacles and setbacks?

empathy

- [ ] am I being attentive to emotional cues?

- [ ] am I truly listening to others?

- [ ] am I being sensitive and understanding of others' perspectives?

- [ ] am I willing to be helpful based on my understanding of others' needs and feelings?

social skills

- [ ] am I sending clear and convincing messages?

- [ ] am I making an effort to negotiate and resolve disagreements?

- [ ] am I initiating, promoting, and managing change?

- [ ] am I inspiring people to do better?

dealing with workplace culture

If you studied abroad during college, you may have gone through what is commonly known as culture shock. You probably didn't feel anything negative at first because you were excited about being in a new country and were looking forward to all the new things you would be experiencing. But after settling in, the honeymoon phase eventually wore off and feelings of anxiety, disorientation, and confusion started to surface. This is because it finally dawned on you how unfamiliar your new surroundings were. Sometimes you weren't sure how to act in certain situations or it may have been difficult for you to communicate effectively. These kinds of experiences could have caused you to feel insecure, powerless, and lost.

Even if you haven't traveled much, these feelings may sound a bit familiar to you because, if you think about it, twentysomethings go through a similar type of cultural change as they make the transition from college to the working world. While you were in college, you spent four or more years in a unique culture that you became quite familiar with. You knew where to go, what to do, and how to do it. But after leaving college, you are thrown into the new culture of the working world and slowly begin to realize that there is a different set of rules and norms to abide by. This can create a sense of helplessness and panic because you may not know how to act in this new environment. As Francisco, a twenty-five-year-old from Kansas City, puts it, "I think one of the most difficult things I had to deal with after college was struggling to learn how to be a professional during my first job. Being professional meant behaving according to a certain set of implicit and explicit norms in the workplace. For example, I made sure to return all voice mails and e-mails within one business day. In college I worked hard when I felt inspired or motivated, often with no regard for what hour of day (or night) or where I was. Since my professors only cared about getting my papers on time, this wasn't a problem. This working style, however, was not consistent with the expectations of my manager—it wasn't 'professional.' The quality of my work mattered greatly and so did the method in which I got my work done. Now I had to plan how my work would get done, be flexible enough to accommodate the schedules and commitments of those working with me, and organize my personal life around the work. This was a big change."

adjusting to a different work environment

"The toughest transition for me after college was realizing how much responsibility I now had at work," says Zach, a twenty-six-year-old from Houston. "I was doing investment banking and I just didn't like it. It was making me entirely miserable. However, unlike college, this wasn't a decision that I could somehow get out of. This wasn't a class that I could withdraw from or abandon after add/drop. This wasn't going to end in a semester. I had made a decision, and I had to take responsibility for it. Unlike college where you are your own master and can somehow explain away anything if you wanted to, I had to just accept this. At school, I'd skip a class and just tell myself it was because I was tired and needed rest or I could catch up on another class. At work, I realized that I had responsibilities toward tons of other people to show up and get my job done regardless of whether I'd had a bad night or maybe even if I was a little under the weather."

As Zach points out, an obvious difference between college and a real job is the change in work protocol. In college, you had the option of doing your homework right away or waiting until the last minute and always had the possibility of talking your way into an extension. You also had long periods of time to get your assignments done, so you could take the time to hang out or take a nap, postponing your work without any real consequences. But in the working world, this usually doesn't fly. In many of the jobs twentysomethings hold, work has to get done the same day, if not the same hour. If you don't do it, a serious reprimand from your boss may be coming your way.

Another difficult adjustment is dealing with a different type of work agenda. In both high school and college there was a specific path to follow that directed us toward a single goal—graduation—with smaller goals, such as doing well on papers and exams, that led up to the long-term goal of attaining our college degree. However, in the working world, there is no underlying directive, no overarching agenda under which recent graduates are supposed to operate. In many jobs there are no clear-cut projects with obvious beginnings and endings and a specific result you are trying to attain. In college we produced a visible end product, such as a paper, laboratory experiments, or exams, and we saw the results of our efforts by getting our grades in a matter of weeks. This allowed us to quickly judge if we were doing a good job or not. But in the working world, many twentysomethings do not produce a product that concretely displays the fruits of their labors and do not get frequent comments about their work. As a result, many twentysomethings feel like they have nothing tangible to look forward to other than a paycheck and are unsure about their work performance because they're not getting the feedback they're accustomed to.

saying hello to the human rainbow

But adjusting to the nine-to-five daily grind is only part of the story of transitioning into a new working world. Because of the spread of free-market ideals around the globe, more people than ever are entering the global marketplace, and this is making for an increasingly diverse business environment. As Thomas Friedman points out in his description of today's global economy, "Globalization 3.0 is not only going to be driven more by individuals but also by a much "more diverse"—nonwestern, nonwhite—group of individuals. In Globalization 3.0 you are going to see every color of the human rainbow take part" (2005a).

Psychologist Christopher Earley from the London Business School and his colleague Soon Ang have found that this diversity is redefining the corporate culture in organizations today. In order to thrive, you must be able to bring intelligence to your awareness of this new culture:

> Foreign cultures are everywhere—in other countries, certainly, but in corporations, vocations, and regions. Interacting with individuals within them demands perceptiveness and adaptability. And the people who have these traits in abundance aren't necessarily the ones who enjoy the greatest social success in familiar settings. Culture Intelligence, or CQ, is the ability to make sense of unfamiliar contexts and then blend in (2003, 1).

What this means for twentysomethings is that using your cultural intelligence to navigate through a world of diverse people and organizations that have their own unique set of habits, norms, and assumptions is a skill that is becoming more valuable in today's global economy.

This is especially true as twentysomethings become more and more mobile. Today, portability means marketability, and in trying to figure out what path to go down, twentysomethings can jump from job to job and never really settle down on one career path. As a result, knowing how to adapt to new organizational cultures is essential if you want to be happy in your new jobs and the places you move to. As Earley and Ang point out:

> In a world where crossing boundaries is routine, CQ becomes a vitally important aptitude and skill, and not just for international bankers and borrowers. Companies, too, have cultures, often very distinctive; anyone who joins a new company spends the first few weeks deciphering its cultural code. Within any large company there are sparring subcultures as well. The sales force can't talk to the engineers, and the PR people lose patience with the lawyers. Departments, divisions, professions, geographical regions—each has a constellation of manners, meanings, histories, and values that will confuse an interloper and cause him or her to stumble. Unless, that is, he or she has a high CQ (2003, 2).

cultivating your culture intelligence

There are a number of psychological techniques that Earley and Ang suggest using to increase your cultural intelligence and make the transition into any working environment a smooth one. The first thing to do is, when you begin a new job, make an effort to learn everything you can about the beliefs, customs, and taboos of that workplace's culture. If there is a training program or orientation, be sure to pay attention not only to what the people say, but also what they do. When you go back to your work setting, ask your coworkers what they thought of the orientation when they took it. Often, you will get a more accurate picture of what the organizational culture is really like from those who are directly in it as opposed to people from the human resources department who are often removed from what you will be experiencing on a daily basis.

Another psychological technique you can use is learning to pay attention to your body language around other people. Earley and Ang have found that:

> you will not disarm your foreign hosts, guests, or colleagues simply by showing you understand their culture; your actions and demeanor must prove that you have already to some extent entered their world. Whether it's the way you shake hands or order coffee, evidence of an ability to mirror the customs and gestures of the people around you will prove that you esteem them well enough to want to be like them (2003, 4).

When you adopt the habits and mannerisms of the people you work with, you will begin to understand them in a most elemental way. As a result, people will start becoming more open and trusting of you.

One other way to improve your cultural intelligence is by using your emotional intelligence to keep your motivation high. As Earley and Ang explain:

Adapting to a new culture includes overcoming obstacles and setbacks. People can only do that if they believe in their own efficacy. If they persevered in the face of challenging situations in the past, their confidence grew. Confidence is always rooted in mastery of a particular task or set of circumstances. A person who doesn't believe herself capable of understanding people from unfamiliar cultures will often give up after her efforts meet with hostility or incomprehension. By contrast, a person with high motivation, upon confronting obstacles, setbacks, or even failure, reengages with greater vigor (2003, 4).

When I spoke to Dr. Earley at a lecture he gave at George Washington University, he mentioned that one of the most important things you can do to adapt to a new culture is increase your self-efficacy as soon as you enter your new environment. One way to do this is by finding five things that you enjoy or that relax you, and then spend the first few weeks mastering them completely. These activities don't necessarily have to be work related. They can be things like finding a place to read the paper and drink coffee, constantly going for a walk around a nice area where you work, or speaking to a coworker you have interesting conversations with. By doing this, you will gradually start becoming more comfortable with your surroundings and develop greater confidence because you will have mastered these things within the context of your new environment. This will then provide you with a foundation of self-efficacy to draw upon as the demands from your job start to increase.

Not only can you do this when you start a new job, but you can also use this technique each time you move to a new city. If you're unfamiliar with the new place you just moved to, spend the first few weeks finding places that you enjoy hanging out at. Become comfortable with the new area and learn to master enjoying your surroundings. This strategy can be extremely helpful if you don't know anyone. What will eventually happen is that you will begin feeling more comfortable, confident, and social when you're out. This will then increase your chances of meeting new people.

creating happiness in any type of work you do

Think of the last time you felt like nothing else in the world mattered. Whatever you were doing at that time, you were so involved in it that everything else seemed to fade into the background of your consciousness. Maybe it was at your job when you were working on an exciting project. Perhaps it was when you were playing some sport and you were making all the right moves or taking all the right shots. Maybe it was when you and your friends were having a deep conversation about the meaning of life. Or maybe you were simply reading a complex book that you just couldn't put down. At that moment, what you were doing, what you felt, and what you thought—all that you were experiencing—was in perfect harmony.

These times when you feel in complete control of your actions and feel a deep sense of exhilaration are what Mihaly Csikszentmihalyi calls *flow experiences* (1990). Contrary to what people usually assume, moments where you feel most alive and fulfilled are not passive or relaxing times like lying on a beach or watching TV.

Although such experiences can certainly be pleasurable, the most fulfilling times in life are when your body and mind are stretched to their limits while trying to accomplish something difficult and valuable.

the ultimate skill-building tool

Csikszentmihalyi has found that there are a number of essential elements involved in the creation of an optimal experience:

> Flow tends to occur when a person's skills are fully involved in overcoming a challenge that is just about manageable. Optimal experience usually involves a fine balance between one's ability to act and the availability of opportunities for action. If challenges are too high, one gets frustrated, worried, and eventually anxious. If challenges are too low relative to one's skills, one gets relaxed, then bored. If both challenge and skills are perceived to be low, one gets to feel apathetic (1996, 30).

In other words, when there is a challenge and you match it with high skills, then you provide yourself a window to become deeply involved in flow and an opportunity to build up your skill levels.

bringing flow to your work

One of your greatest opportunities to create flow is at your job. Your work can provide a situation where your skills are adequately challenged by the task at hand, there is a goal to be achieved and a clear set of rules in which to get it done, as well as feedback along the way to show how you are performing. Sometimes, however, your job may not provide you with all these ingredients. In these instances, you will have to take it upon yourself to create the conditions needed to enter flow. In fact, the ability to create flow at work is one of the most important skills that companies are looking for today. If you are a person who finds challenges that need to be dealt with, sets your own goals, and directs yourself in such a way that creates productivity within the organization, then you are bound to easily find a job in today's marketplace. Below are the elements to look for in creating flow in your work.

Constantly challenge yourself. The first step in creating flow is finding activities that require a significant use of your skills and that you have a chance of completing. People report optimal experiences most often when they are involved in activities that are goal-directed and require investment in their psychic energy. It is when your skills are fully involved in overcoming a challenge that is just about manageable that you have the best chance of entering flow. So try to find activities at work where you will be challenged but not overwhelmed.

Become one with the experience. When your skills are well matched with the challenges of an activity at work, your attention will sharpen and quickly you will find yourself absorbed by the project. This is the point when you can enter the flow zone and become one with the activity. At this point, all your attention is focused on the relevant stimuli, and you become so involved in what you're trying to accomplish that you stop being aware of yourself as separate from the actions you are performing and everything seems to become automatic and effortless.

But as Csikszentmihalyi has found, while it seems that the flow experience is being done automatically and without much effort, it in fact paradoxically requires a significant amount of effort—in physical exertion and/or highly disciplined mental activity. If you have a lapse in concentration, flow will quickly disappear. If you begin questioning why you're doing every single thing you are doing, you will most likely make a mistake. You achieve flow when you let your mind and body perform harmoniously and let the action carry you forward to the achievement of your goal.

Set clear goals that provide feedback. Another important factor involved in achieving such a complete involvement in your work are goals that provide clear feedback. Being able to see how you are performing is important because it allows you the opportunity to alter your actions to continue performing at peak efficiency. However, sometimes projects at work do not have clear-cut goals and clear feedback isn't always available. In these cases, you will need to create your own goals and make sure that they allow you to gauge your progress. Otherwise you will find them difficult to enjoy.

This kind of goal setting at work can be challenging also because you're not used to it. While growing up, you never really had to create your own goals or make sure you got feedback because this was taken care of by school. You always got feedback from your teachers, either in grade or verbal and/or written form, and you were able to make adjustments based on these comments in order to move forward. But in the working world, goals can often be ambiguous. Sometimes you can work on projects that have no real beginning or ending, and you may not get regular feedback from your supervisors. If your job bores you, your paycheck probably won't be an adequate goal to motivate you onward. That is why it is important to take it upon yourself to look for ways, even if they are not visible, to create order and rules for all the activities you engage in during your twenties.

Pay attention. During the course of the day you can be barraged by fleeting thoughts that may distract you and cloud your mind. What your attention does is act as a filter between what happens in the outside world and how you experience it within your mind. For example, say you have a manager who is belligerent, constantly yelling at you, and is just plain mean. How much this situation affects you will depend much more on how much attention you give the situation than on what actually happens to you. The more attention you give to the hurtful things your manager says, the more real it will become, and the more negativity will enter your consciousness.

This ability to channel your attention is essential for creating flow because activities that produce enjoyment are, by their very nature, challenging and therefore require you to focus your attention on what you are doing in that moment. The ability to focus your attention means that you are able to control what you experience and thus, control the quality of your life. As Csikszentmihalyi explains:

> Some people learn to use this resource efficiently while others can waste it. The mark of a person who is in control of consciousness is the ability to focus it at will, to be oblivious to distractions, to concentrate for as long as it takes to achieve a goal, and not longer. And the person who can do this usually enjoys the normal course of everyday life (1990, 31).

Learn to get control and let go. One of the most peculiar aspects of flow is not worrying about losing control while at the same time being in complete control of the situation. This feeling is what produces the exhilaration that is essential to optimal experience. This sense of control is also one of the most powerful forces for producing psychological growth and strengthening your vision of self. As we talked about in chapter 1, your self-efficacy is the confidence you have in your ability to handle the challenges you face in life. As you experience more flow experiences, you begin pushing your skills and being to develop a better sense of control, thus increasing your self-efficacy. We also saw in chapter 4 that one of the main reasons twentysomethings become depressed is because they develop a sense of helplessness after college. This perceived sense of not being in control of your environment can create a feeling of being ineffective. What creating flow experiences does is increase your resilience by constantly increasing your skills and self-confidence.

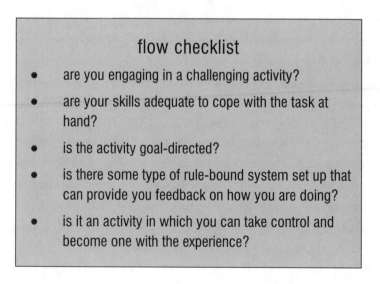

flow checklist

- are you engaging in a challenging activity?
- are your skills adequate to cope with the task at hand?
- is the activity goal-directed?
- is there some type of rule-bound system set up that can provide you feedback on how you are doing?
- is it an activity in which you can take control and become one with the experience?

books you will love

Working with Emotional Intelligence (1998) by Daniel Goleman. The author uses his years of working with organizations around the world to explain why emotional intelligence is becoming the backbone of success in business today and provides a practical guide on how you can integrate emotional intelligence into your work life.

A Whole New Mind: Moving from the Information Age to the Conceptual Age (2005) by Daniel Pink. One of the most important books you will ever read when it comes to understanding how and why the world is changing economically and culturally to create the new working world twentysomethings transition into after graduation. A great resource describing the types of skills that are becoming essential in the twenty-first century. A must read! Check out the Pink blog at www.danpink.com.

Flow: The Psychology of Optimal Experience (1990) by Mihaly Csikszentmihalyi (pronounced "chick-SENT-me-high"). A major contributor to the positive psychology movement through years of happiness research. Csikszentmihalyi provides a road map for getting into "the zone" and finding fulfillment at work as well as in every other aspect of your life.

The World Is Flat: A Brief History of the Twenty-first Century (2005b) by Thomas Friedman. A great book on how the political-economic events in the latter half of the twentieth century have led to globalization and fundamental changes in how we will conduct our work lives in the twenty-first century.

Cultural Intelligence: Individual Interactions Across Cultures (2003) by P. Christopher Earley and Soon Ang. While academic in nature, this book illuminates a much-needed skill in today's global economy.

Don't Send a Resume: And Other Contrarian Rules to Help Land a Great Job (2001) by Jeffrey Fox and *What Color Is Your Parachute? 2006: A Practical Manual for Job-Hunters and Career-Changers* (2005) by Richard Bolles and Mark Bolles. Two of the best books out there for learning how to increase your chances of getting the job you want.

chapter 6

what kind of people do you want in your life?

Intimate relationships cannot substitute for a life
plan. But to have any meaning or viability at all,
a life plan must include intimate relationships.
—Harriet Lerner

"I definitely think that it's more difficult finding new friends now,
compared to college," says twenty-five-year-old Thomas. "In Washington, DC, it may not be as bad as other places, but after graduation
it's a much more diverse world than college was. It takes much more
time and effort to find someone who's on the same page as you,
whereas in college you would find yourself in the same classes, or
going to the same parties, or going to sporting events with people
who had similar interests. There are bars and things like that that

attract similar types of people, but it's just not quite as conducive to meeting people as it was in college."

As almost any twentysomething will attest to, it becomes much harder to meet people after the social world of our educational system fades away when we leave college. School provided what seemed to be endless opportunities to meet a wide variety of people who were the same age and had similar interests and goals. In college, you could meet new people in classes that changed each semester, in an array of organizations and clubs, at various social activities, and at parties on the weekends. You also had the dining hall and dorms where you could talk for hours on end to help solidify the friendships you were forming. And because you lived the flexible college schedule, you could stay up all night getting to know other people and could either skip class the next day or take a long nap after class to recover. But this all ends come graduation time, leaving you without any real social system to depend on during your postcollege years.

we're no longer living like chia pets

After you grab your diploma and begin the rest of your life outside of academia, one of the first things you probably realized was how much your social life changes. In many ways, this change reminds me of a Chia Pet. You've all seen the commercials—Cha, Cha, Cha, Chia!— and getting your Chia Pet to grow is pretty easy. All you have to do is get the right ingredients, mix them up, spread them over the surface of the your favorite ceramic animal, add some nourishing water and sunlight, and watch it grow. Well, a similar thing happens during college, where you gather the proper students, mix them up, spread them around campus, add some nourishing classes, organizations, social events, and alcohol, let some time pass, and boom—watch all the friendships and casual relationships blossom.

One of the major reasons why Chia Pets and campus relationships seem to bloom so effortlessly is because all the right ingredients necessary for their growth are put together by some external entity. Now, in the case of the Chia Pet, what would happen if you didn't have the right ingredients? What if you didn't mix the ingredients properly and put them in the right environment to grow but, rather, spread them around haphazardly? What if the proper nourishment was not given to them? You would see little or no growth. Well, after graduation twentysomethings are scattered about amongst countless other people in the working world, with the old classroom, organizations, and dining halls quickly replaced by bars and clubs. In this new world, there is no longer an outside entity to make sure that you're surround by the right people or are comfortable in your new social environments.

This is not to say that the types of people you knew simply disappeared after college. Rather, all these individuals are thrown into a sea of people who are different ages, have different goals and purposes, and may not fit too well with you on a number of levels. Although many twentysomethings said that in some ways it's cool to be in a world with a wide variety of people, they also said that it can often be difficult to find common ground because people living in the real world have various careers, different social and personal interests, and many times are at different stages in their lives. As a result, it can be a challenge to make a connection similar to the ones you made in college, where everyone's life centered on the common pursuit of getting an education.

losing your core

What can often compound the difficulty in adjusting to this new diversity of people is the loss of your college friends when you separate and move to all parts of the country. Many times new jobs can take you and your friends to different cities far away from each other. This can often leave twentysomethings without a core group of friends. Raul, a twenty-six-year-old from San Diego, says, "I moved three thousand miles away from my family and friends for my new job. I came to the West Coast knowing only one person. In my first year at work I was very lonely. I had the impression that all my college friends living in Boston and New York were having wonderful times hanging out with each other, and I felt pretty lost out here on the West Coast. A consequence of this was that I traveled back east a lot. During the spring of my first year out here, I took about eight or nine trips back east. Sometimes I would be out of L.A. for two or three weekends a month. Obviously that wasn't a good idea either financially or emotionally. I've now been in L.A. for almost three years and only after about a year and a half did I start to feel like the people I wanted to be with live close to me."

Because of the major change of going from a close-knit community enclosed by the college campus to a divided group of friends scattered all over the country, twentysomethings said they can have a tough time adjusting on their own and, at times, experience intense feelings of loneliness. "When I moved to my new job, it totally reminded me of freshman year of college—lots of nervous energy as people go through the repeated questioning of where everyone's from, what they're going to be doing—all with the thought in the back of their mind, 'Will I find people I can really click with?'" says

Sarah, a twenty-five-year-old from Houston. "I left Boston at the end of May and then spent a week at home before driving down to Houston. Two days later and I was finally there and, well, I felt a little overwhelmed and crazed about the fact that I was slated to be at this job for two years. I felt that sort of claustrophobia that can be almost paralyzing. I knew in my head that I'd get over the feeling, find a place to live, and of course, friends to hang out with. But deep in my heart there was this fear that I wouldn't find anyone to click with—and that really freaked me out. I had grown accustomed to having several small groups of friends while always keeping a core group of friends to support me. As I went into perhaps one of the hardest jobs I've had yet, I was scared that I wouldn't have the friends I would need."

adjusting to a new life schedule

Not only do you lose your core group of friends after college, but you also lose the freedom and flexibility to hang out with the friends you do have whenever you want. This rigidity that working-world hours impose on your time can have a major impact on how you prioritize friendships. After finishing up ten or twelve hours at the job, it can be hard to go out after work and meet people because you are so tired from the workday. Some twentysomethings I spoke to told me that often they would rather just curl up on the couch and "veg" in front of the TV instead of hitting the noisy and crowded bars.

But this infrequency of going out to meet new people can put extra pressure to form friendships and social circles when the opportunity presents itself, causing you to possibly hide how you are truly feeling by acting happier and more energetic than you really are. Says Joanna, a twenty-five-year-old from Detroit: "We are all so busy and there is always so much going on that it feels like people don't have the time to deal with others people's problems. And if you don't act happy, who will want to hang out with you? I mention the issue of time because that seems to be the biggest difference between college and postcollege work life. In college, I had three hours in the middle of the day to hang out with friends, complain, and talk about problems, plans, goals, and worries. But now, I don't have that much time to talk about problems with anyone other than my best friend or significant other, and sometimes it feels like I am putting just another burden on them. In the same vein, because of time constraints, I don't see friends as much, and the less you see someone, the more pressure you feel to act happy and pleasant when you're around them."

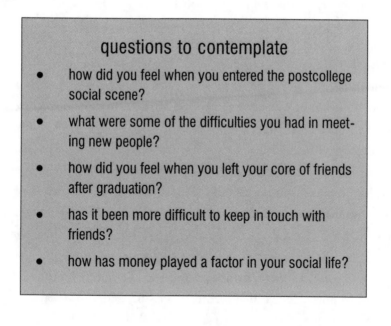

questions to contemplate

- how did you feel when you entered the postcollege social scene?

- what were some of the difficulties you had in meeting new people?

- how did you feel when you left your core of friends after graduation?

- has it been more difficult to keep in touch with friends?

- how has money played a factor in your social life?

no money, mo problems

Another major obstacle that twentysomethings said they encounter in meeting new people are the low-paying jobs they often work in after graduation. Most twentysomethings are not making the big bucks after college and quickly find out that this can put a serious obstacle in the way of making a connection with others. "When I started my first job, I got paid twenty-three thousand dollars a year," says Renee, a twenty-three-year-old consultant, "which made it really difficult to live in a city like DC. With student loans, rent, and other bills, these costs pretty much caused me to just spend a lot of time in my apartment when I first graduated. When you see how much your actual paycheck is after taxes, it's a shock to the system. I remember when I got my first check—my stomach just turned. I could have gotten an additional job, but the hours I was already working made it impossible for me to get one during the week, and my first job wore me down so much that it was really important for me to be able to relax during my weekends. In order to try to make my money last, I wouldn't do much during the weekends, which made it a bit more difficult to meet people. I don't really remember anyone during college talking about what to expect financially other than the student loan people having a class where they talked to us about ways to make sure we don't default on our student loans. It can be such a cycle—you don't make enough money, so you have an inexpensive apartment in a bad neighborhood, or you can't afford to go out and then can't meet any new people when you're living in an entirely new area. Then if you're stuck in your apartment, you at least want to have nice things to make you feel comfortable, so you spend money on things you don't need. Money is definitely a big worry."

a rough dating world

"Dating in the twenty-first century, postcollege ... hmmm ... Well, I guess I'd describe it as a roller coaster that's mostly been going downhill," says Chris, a twenty-six-year-old from Boston. "When I graduated, I was still in a long-term relationship. While there were other problems with our relationship, one of the hardest aspects of staying together after college was dating long distance. In the end, I broke up with her and a major part of this was because we were so far apart. I think that has been one of the toughest aspects of dating in postcollege life for me—distance combined with personal aspirations. People graduating from college usually have plans for themselves, and those plans don't always necessarily work well with mating. All I know is that I find dating to be a major challenge postcollege, period! I have no money, I have no time to date, and I am never meeting people my own age I would even consider dating."

As Chris explains, dating during the turbulent twenties can often become confusing, hectic, or in many cases, nonexistent. This is because ever since your first day of school, your mating life has almost always taken place in some type of educational setting. In secondary school, you were constantly surrounded by fellow teens and could easily get to know them in classes, during clubs and sports, or at after-school events. Then you were off to college, which in many ways was an extension of high school with less parental control and more freedom. Along with this new liberation, you were surrounded by a ton of people you had a lot in common with. And although the admissions committee didn't have this specifically in mind when selecting students, they actually helped find good sexual matches even before you arrived on campus by choosing other students who, even if they came from different backgrounds, had very similar traits, interests, and goals. The rules of the college mating game were pretty straightforward—hook up, hang out, or get into a joined-at-the-hip relationship. Operating within these college norms, you could get to know potential partners while you ate in the dining hall, on study dates in the library, in campus organizations, or simply just hanging out in the dorms till the wee hours of the morning—not to mention that the majority of these "dates" were free!

But this changes as soon as the mating world you lived in for your entire postpubescent lives vanishes and you're thrust into an unfamiliar world with a new set of rules for dating, sex, and love. After college, the interactive classroom that surrounded you with people your own age is quickly replaced by an often-isolated and mundane office job with coworkers who are often twice your age. The common pursuit of getting an education that bound us all together disappears and leaves us with no real communal place to meet potential mates with similar interests and goals. The bar and club scene soon becomes a substitute for the dining hall and campus organizations, and the social events that used to be free in college now cost money that a lot of twentysomethings simply don't have.

questions to contemplate

- how has your dating life changed since graduation?
- has it gotten better or worse? why?
- what have you done to meet new people?
- have these methods been successful?

the new social support systems— urban tribes

Because we are always moving to new cities for our jobs, most likely not living close to our families, and waiting longer to get married, there is no real support system that is readily available to us after graduation. As a result, twentysomethings are finding others ways to create the sense of community that disappears after college. One way they are doing this is described in Ethan Watters' book *Urban Tribes: A Generation Redefines Friendship, Family, and Commitment* (2003). Watters has found that young people today are adapting to their social environments after college by establishing strong bonds with friends who often live in the same city. Because more and more twentysomethings are staying in school longer, entering demanding careers, living away from home, and delaying marriage, they are forming a new type of social entity to take the place of more traditional forms of family. Some of the major characteristics that Watters describes of urban tribes are:

Intense loyalty: Just like a family by blood, there is an intense loyalty with the members, providing a strong support system.

Shared routines and rituals: This can take the form of regular dinners together, group vacations, parties, and get-togethers on holidays.

A sense of "barn raising": Members are there to always lend a helping hand with moving, painting, or creating gardens in the backyard.

Love gossip: The group seems to always be talking about what is happening in the lives of all the members of the tribe—especially when it comes to relationships.

Defined roles: People seem to fall into certain roles within the tribe. This may be the result of people playing to their strengths. For example, someone may be the organizer, another the advice giver, the other the creator and handyperson.

Dating rules: In some tribes, there will be dating within the group, while in others there is an unspoken or spoken rule against forming relationships or having casual sex within the tribe.

But even though most tribes usually have these things in common, Watters found that urban tribes can vary greatly:

> The size, composition, rules, and rituals of these groups varied dramatically. Many people describe lives lived bouncing between two or more core groups. One group had formed around college friends, while another had formed in a workplace. Some groups ... had several dozen members, while others described tribes of three or four members that had been together less than a year. Some were all of one gender and race, while others were remarkably diverse." Watters went on to conclude that, "The complexity and heterogeneous nature of these accounts was staggering. It appeared that the lives of young adults were varying in every imaginable way" (2003, 8).

While groups of friends have existed in the past, what is unique about twentysomethings today is that because of the new lifestyle they are living, urban tribes are becoming the new family of the twenties and can provide a much-needed sense of community in a time of such instability.

how can you meet new people?

While it may not be as easy to meet people now compared to college, there are a number of things you can do to increase your chances of meeting new people, an urban tribe, or someone to date. However, there are a few things to keep in mind when trying to make new friends or find potential mates during the turbulent twenties. First, the chances of meeting lots of people you really connect with automatically decreases after college by virtue of the fact that you are now in an ocean of other people who most likely will not be a good fit for you. People who share the same purpose and view of life may turn up less often than they did in college, so don't get down if it takes some time to find a great friend or urban tribe after college.

Second, don't give up if you meet someone but don't make a connection with them right off the bat. If you don't become best friends within the first week of meeting them, don't sweat it. It was much easier to form quick and intense relationships in college because of proximity, the type of people we were surrounded by, and the kind lifestyle we led. Friendships and romantic relationships usually progress much slower in the working world.

Another thing you always have to keep in mind is that you're never going to meet anybody if you don't make an effort. Unless you are willing to muster up the courage to go talk to people and see if there is a connection, you won't make any friends or get dates. This means that going up to people, making good conversation, exchanging phone numbers, and making the first call is something you will have to do. For a lot of twentysomethings, this may be the first time you've been forced to make friends on your own without the Chia Pet social world. It can be tough and even a little bit scary. You may feel like you're bothering or imposing on people, but you'll never know if you never try. Now let's look at what twentysomethings said were the best ways to meet new friends and dates after graduation.

Clubs or sports leagues. Almost every town and city has a number of clubs and sports activities that you can join. Although they may not always be filled with nothing but twentysomethings, most likely there will be some young people there. There is also the possibility that the company you work for has a softball team or some other type of sports club. This is a great way to get to know coworkers, and even if there aren't a lot of young people, there may be a few, and it is very likely that they know other twentysomethings you can hang with. The most important thing is to do something you are interested in. If you join a club or team that you don't like just to meet people, then you may actually hurt your chances of getting to know others because you will be unhappy while you're interacting with them. Simply put, you need to have fun both in the activity and with the people, otherwise it's probably just a waste of your time.

Volunteering. If you want a change of pace from the bar scene, volunteering is a good way to go. There are a number of national groups such as

Habitat for Humanity or numerous local groups that you can find in your city paper that provide you with the opportunity to interact with a variety of people while doing a good deed. There are also organizations that cater to singles (such as Single Volunteers) that have a specific agenda in mind but aren't too much of a meat market. Clubs like these usually have a minimum number of single people for each activity, so you usually get a good number of young people to interact with. For more information, go to www.SingleVolunteers.org.

Take a class. There are a variety of classes that you can take to meet new people. They usually don't cost much money and are a great way to interact with people because you usually have to work in groups to accomplish whatever you're doing. You can take a cooking class, painting class, dance class, or go to wine tasting events. There is also the option to take classes at a community college or university in the area if you have the money. There are professional classes as well as academic classes you can take. My experience with this is people are usually very friendly and the educational environment often lends itself to getting to know people very well. Plus, you can all go out for a drink after class.

Social networking. Just as networking is the best way for you to get a job, it's also one of the best ways for you to meet new people. You can do this anywhere, but one of the best places I've found to network is going out with your coworkes for happy hour. Not only will you meet people outside your department, but usually your coworkers will invite some of their friends to come along. However, there is one word of advice: try not to let the evening turn into a gossip session about work. If this happens, try to steer the conversation onto other topics, especially if there are people that don't work with you there. Then you can find out more about the people themselves and see if there is a potential to make a connection with some of them.

managing your relationships with emotional intelligence

In chapter 5 we talked about the importance of using your emotional intelligence when interacting with your coworkers. But there are in fact many other relationships in your life that can benefit from your emotional intelligence. Let's take a look at how you can use this intelligence to create better personal relationships during your twenties.

awareness of your self and others

Whenever you encounter someone, how you relate to them and the quality of that interaction will be heavily determined by how aware you are of your emotions. For example, if someone has treated you badly in the past, your awareness of your feelings will determine how the next encounter with them will turn out. If you see them, are taken over by anger, but remain unaware that this is what you are feeling, most likely you will have a hostile confrontation with them. On the other hand, if you acknowledge and understand what you're feeling, you can accept your emotions and make a conscious effort to prevent them from negatively affecting your experience with that person.

Your self-awareness also helps you manage your relationships by providing you with the necessary information to modify what to say, how to say it, and what type of body language to use. If you are unaware of how you feel in the presence of other people it will be difficult, if not impossible, to make decisions about what is the best way to interact with them. I am sure you have met someone who seems to have few social skills or is very uneasy in a basic social setting. Oftentimes, the reason people act like this is because they don't know what they are feeling in the presence of others and therefore don't know what is appropriate for the situation.

Other times, people may be aware of their emotions, but they try to ignore or numb what they are feeling. I'm sure you have seen this with a person who starts dating someone who is not good for them. They may tell you that for some reason they have a bad feeling about the person, but don't explore their gut reaction further or simply choose to ignore it and continue on with the relationship. But eventually their lack of awareness comes at a cost when the person they are dating eventually makes them miserable. It's not only important to pay attention to your inner signals, but to use that information to make more intelligent decisions about your relationships. This can help prevent unnecessary suffering and allow you the opportunity to invest your time and energy in more enjoyable experiences.

check yourself before you wreck yourself

But we also have to be realistic: relationships do not always go smoothly, nor are you always going to be able to read people well enough in advance to prevent them from making you feel bad. With two or more people come different sets of likes and dislikes, different sets of interests and goals, and different personalities. As a result, there is bound to be conflict in relationships, and during these times you may not have the opportunity to control whether you will have a negative emotional response to a specific social situation. But even if you can't predict your emotions, you certainly have the power to control how you handle what you feel and more importantly, how long it lasts. One of the ways you can do this is by learning to take a step back during heated or stressful times, keep your impulses in check, and look at the situation from all angles to make sure that what you are feeling is appropriate to the situation.

I am sure you have encountered people who seem to always be on an emotional roller coaster. You never know how they are going to react to something, and one reason they seem to be so out of control is because their emotions are dependent on what happens in their external environment rather than on their ability to regulate what they are feeling. This inability to check themselves before they let their emotions take over is a major sign that that person is lacking intelligence about their emotions.

One thing to keep in mind is that emotional regulation does not mean that you are repressing how you are feeling. When you manage your emotions, you are not controlling *what* you're feeling, but rather are making the conscious effort to control *how you are expressing* what you're feeling.

"I feel your pain"

While many people made fun of Bill Clinton when he said this to a group of African-Americans, he in fact was displaying a skill that human relationships are built upon: the ability to empathize. What Clinton was trying to do was show that he was making an effort to see things from their perspective and was responding to their concerns. It is this ability to understand where other people are coming from, as well as taking an interest in what they are feeling, that is one of the most basic ways we relate to one another. As Goleman explains:

> Sensing what others feel without their saying it captures the essence of empathy. Others rarely tell us in words what they feel; instead they tell us in their tone of voice, facial expression, or other nonverbal ways. The ability to sense these subtle communications builds on more basic competencies, particularly self-awareness and self-control. Without the ability to sense our own feelings—or to keep them from swamping us—we will be hopelessly out of touch with the moods of others (1998, 135).

One of the basic ways we empathize is by picking up on the facial expression of others. For example, psychologist Elaine Hatfield and her colleagues found that when you see someone who is happy, it evokes the same emotion inside you (1994). This is also true of anger, sadness, and almost any other emotion. Hatfield has found that to the extent that you mimic the pace, posture, and facial expressions of someone, you will begin feeling what they are feeling.

One way you can increase your ability to empathize is by becoming an "active" listener. I am sure that you have met someone who cannot or simply does not listen to what you are saying. These kinds of people usually come off as uncaring or indifferent, and if you do not want to be perceived in the same light, you have to make a conscious effort to be open to what people are saying at the time they are saying it. A good way to do this is by restating in your own words what someone is saying to you. Not only will you make the other person feel like you are listening, but by restating it in your own words you will develop a better understanding of what they are trying to communicate and where they're coming from.

social skills

Think about a time when you were not feeling so great and then a friend came over to cheer you up. When you saw them, they had a smile on their face and you quickly felt better. Or think of a time when you were with a group of friends having a great time and then a friend of a friend who is always anxious or in a bad mood joins you and completely brings the mood of the whole group down. In both instances, your feelings or the group's feelings quickly changed. This is because of a fundamental characteristic of emotions: they are contagious.

The exchange of emotions is often so subtle that we don't take notice of them. However, you may want to start paying greater attention to this psychological process because it can have a powerful impact on how you relate to others. For example, in a study by researchers Howard Friedman and Ronald Riggio, three strangers were instructed to sit quietly in a circle for two minutes. Then at the end of two minutes the researchers checked the emotional pulse of the participants. What they found was that the person who was the most expressive had transmitted his or her mood to the other two people. Friedman and Riggio found that regardless of whether the most expressive person was feeling happy, angry, or sad, in every session the people with the strongest show of emotion infected the other two people with what they were feeling at the time (1981).

What this means is that during every single social encounter, you have the ability to influence how other people are feeling by transmitting emotional signals—and you can be affected by emotional signals that are sent by others. As a result, the more adept you are at reading and understanding the emotional messages of others, the better able you will be at controlling the signals you send and receive. So if you enter a situation where someone is in a bad mood, instead of letting them get you down, you can actually make them feel better by displaying signs of happiness. This ability to soothe the emotions of other people is one of the most important ways in which you can manage your relationships.

To increase your emotional intelligence in your relationships, you can use the questions from chapter 5 and simply apply them to your personal life.

a time for exploring yourself and others

In his book *Emerging Adulthood: The Winding Road from the Late Teens Through the Twenties* (2004), Jeffrey Arnett describes this period during our twenties as a time of exploring personal relationships more than any other time in life. Arnett has found that most twentysomethings report feeling the need to try out a wide variety of relationships during these years and not feeling ready to make a commitment to others. Psychologists W. Andrew Collins and Manfred van Dulmen from the University of Minnesota suggest that this desire to delay commitment is because of the balancing act twentysomethings go through between exploring one's self and how others fit into this period of self-discovery (2005).

This delay can certainly be seen when you look at when twentysomethings are getting married today. During the 1940s until the 1970s, the nationwide average age for getting married was about twenty-one for women and twenty-three for men. Today, the age for getting married has risen to about twenty-five for women and twenty-seven for men (U.S. Census Bureau 2000).

One of the main reasons why twentysomethings are waiting so long to commit is because there is now much more of an emphasis on getting higher levels of education, leading more of them to go to graduate school directly or soon after college. There has also been a new emphasis on finding a career that brings fulfillment, with twentysomethings wanting to experiment with a variety of jobs before settling down into a serious relationship. Then there is the fact that twentysomethings may be working long hours to get ahead in the jobs and the lack of time causes them to evaluate their relationships much differently than they did during college. As Cathleen, a twenty-eight-year-old from Albuquerque, New Mexico, explains, "Since it seems like I have no time, I am much more particular about who I get involved with. I realize more and more how relationships are a serious investment of time and energy, and I have to make sure that the person I get involved with is worth it. I have done the whole hook-up thing and am bored with it, so now I am more interested in whether interactions will turn into a meaningful relationship. I always ask myself questions like, 'Do they have potential and are they ambitious (not just financially)? Are they intelligent, can they keep up with me, will I get bored with them quickly? Do they inspire me?' During college, I think it was easy to meet someone you had a lot in common with. You could hang out all the time studying, spend the night at each other's dorm, and you really didn't become too serious because there were so many other things to focus on and it seemed like you were living in a play world. But as I realize how limited my time is, I don't want to waste a single second of it. I think this allows me to utilize my time in a much more fulfilling way, but at the same time it can put a little bit of pressure to find 'the one.'"

the most important relationship of all

One interesting thing about Cathleen's experience that is quite common among twentysomethings today is that she very much takes into account the type of person she is as well as the context in which she is living in to help her determine who she wants to bring into her life. When it comes to figuring out the type of people you want in your life, you essentially are asking, "Given who I am, what are the kinds of people I would like to have in my life, and what do I expect from those relationships?" Or in the case of romantic relationships, "Given who I am, what kind of person would I like to have as a partner for the rest of my life?"

As psychologist Eric Erickson suggested during his study of adolescence, before you can truly be intimate with other people, you must resolve the issues you have with your identity (1994). So whether it is finding a good group of friends, someone fun to date, or the love of your life, before you are able to fully answer the question, "What kind of people do I want in my life?" you have to first answer, "What kind of person am I?" Whenever you relate to others, especially on an intimate level, you always do it from the context of who you are as an individual. As a result, in order to form personal relationships that are meaningful and have a positive effect on your life, it is necessary to have a basic sense of who you are.

focusing on you

One of the themes running throughout this book has been that your twenties is one of the greatest times in your life for self-exploration, and as you engage in this journey of self-discovery, you enter a time that is extremely self-focused. In fact, the period after college may be the most selfish time of your life because you are spending a great deal of energy trying to improve who you are and figure out who you want to become. This automatically requires that you begin focusing more on yourself and what makes you happy. We have also seen that if you don't make a conscious effort to shift your focus to your vision of self, it is virtually impossible to create the kind of life you want to build for yourself during your twenties.

But you may feel awkward saying that you are being selfish during this period of life. We typically associate selfishness with people behaving badly. Therefore, saying that you are increasing the focus on yourself has the potential to make you feel guilty. But let's take a moment to think about this: Is there any real reason why you should feel guilty for being self-focused? Should you feel guilty for wanting to improve the quality of your life by concentrating more on yourself? Is it bad to figure out what is the best way to support your life by your own efforts and achieve happiness as a result of those efforts? Certainly not, and anyone who tells you that being concerned with your own interest is selfish is suggesting that the desire to live life on your own terms, finding happiness and fulfillment, is bad.

Now, I have brought this up in the context of figuring out what kind of relationships you want during your twenties because before you can develop deep, intimate relationships with others, it is necessary to develop a healthy relationship with yourself first. This is because the more you learn about yourself and make an effort to improve who you are, then the more you have to offer people. As you work to make yourself a better person, the better you can relate to others, help them, inspire them, and influence their lives in a positive manner.

However, I would like to point out that focusing more on yourself does not mean you only think about you and no one else. We do not live in a vacuum, and your actions have an impact on other people. If you choose to ignore this fact, then you may alienate and hurt people who are important to you. And if you think about it, is it really in your own self-interest to ignore your valuable relationships? These relationships are of great value to you and a source of support, and if you snub them, it will have a negative effect on your happiness. So by thinking about how people important to you feel and making sure they are happy, you are acting in your self-interest. On the flip side, your friends and family have to understand that you and you alone live inside your body, you and you alone are the one who feels and thinks for you. Therefore, you need to continue to focus on how you can improve *your* life. Those who really care will support you during this process.

books you will love

Urban Tribes: A Generation Redefines Friendship, Family, and Commitment (2003) **by Ethan Watters.** The origin of the term "urban tribes" and a good discussion about how the nature of young people's relationships are changing due to the new lifestyles we are leading today. An enjoyable read! Check out his site at www.urbantribes.net.

The Art of Living Consciously: The Power of Awareness to Transform Everyday Life (1999) **by Nathaniel Branden.** A great book on how to become comfortable being by yourself and increase your level of self-awareness in every aspect of your life.

conclusion

When you cannot make up your mind which of two evenly balanced courses of action you should take— choose the bolder.—William Joseph Slim

When I first came up with the idea of writing *The Turbulent Twenties Survival Guide*, one of the ideas that excited me the most was the day I would finally get my book published. For the first few months, I thought about how good it would feel to see it in bookstores and how my life would change as many new opportunities arose from its publication. I was writing nonstop during that time. However, a few months after I started, I soon found myself struggling to stay focused. I was not writing consistently, and what I did write was not coming out the way I had hoped. I became extremely annoyed and frustrated. Something was going on inside me that I had to figure out, so I stopped my writing and took some time to explore why I was feeling this way.

What I soon realized was that even though having my book published was exciting and motivating, it wasn't enough. I needed something more. As I thought about what that "more" was, I tried picturing what it would actually be like when the book was finally published. I knew part of me would be enjoying the achievement and the possibilities it would open up, but I also realized that another part of me would be someplace else—I would be thinking about the next book I was going to write. And then in the future when that one was published, I would be thinking about the next one. What I quickly understood at that moment was that even though the peaks of our final achievements are moments to be cherished, in the whole scheme of things they are only a small part of life. The reality is that the majority of our twenties and beyond are not going to be spent enjoying these moments, but rather most of your life will be experienced at the *process* level of creating those moments.

In reflecting back on this realization along with what I learned from the thousands of interviews and conversations with twenty-somethings and all the psychological research I have reviewed, I came to one basic conclusion about the psychology of life after college: the purpose of the twenties is all about learning how to find happiness in the journey. It's about learning to enjoy the process of taking the new vision of self you have inside your mind and giving it shape, meaning, and purpose in the outside world. While the moments of achievement in the future will be amazing, life is happening now, at this moment. If you're unable to enjoy it each day, whatever the situation you are in, then there is no reason to expect that your feelings will change after you attain some end goal.

This skill is especially important at work. So much of your new life is going to be spent earning a living, so it's vital to find something you greatly enjoy. But as we have seen, this is not always the case for many twentysomethings. However, even if you are not working in your dream job, you have seen throughout the book the many ways in which you can create happiness from what seems to be a mundane or ordinary situation. By learning to create flow and remain positive and realistic about your work situation, you can learn to stay connected with what you are doing and change the parts of your job that aren't especially interesting or exciting. Of course, there will always be times when we have to do things that aren't interesting to us. But if you learn to turn these kinds of situations into opportunities to learn and experience flow, then life during your twenties will become infinitely more interesting.

This isn't to say that it is wrong to look ahead, either. You certainly need goals and a vision of the future to guide your thoughts and actions. However, this period in life is also about finding a balance between the journey and the end destination. It's about learning to plan ahead without sacrificing what you are experiencing in the moment; about enjoying the present without becoming oblivious to the future.

What will eventually determine this balance? It is the direction you decide to travel down during your postcollege years. Will you choose the road of randomness and chance or the one of living mindfully, purposefully, and relying on your psychological intelligence and vision of self to guide you through the turbulent twenties? The one basic question you have to ask yourself now is, "Which path am I going to travel down?" Good luck, and enjoy every part of finding the answer.

references

Arnett, Jeffrey Jensen. 2004. *Emerging Adulthood: The Winding Road from the Late Teens Through the Twenties.* New York: Oxford University Press.

Arnett, Jeffrey Jensen, and Jennifer Lynn Tanner, eds. 2005. *Emerging Adults in America: Coming of Age in the Twenty-first Century.* Washington, DC: American Psychological Association.

Babyak, Michael A., James A. Blumenthal, Steve Herman, Parinda Khatri, Murali Doraiswamy, Kathleen Moore, W. Edward Craighead, Teri T. Baldewicz, and K. Ranga Krishnan. 2000. Exercise treatment for major depression: Maintenance of therapeutic benefit at 10 months. *Psychosomatic Medicine* 62(5):633–638.

Blumenthal, James A., Michael A. Babyak, Kathleen A. Moore, W. Edward Craighead, Steve Herman, Parinda Khatri, Robert Waugh, et al. 1999. Effects of exercise training on older patients with major depression. *Archives of Internal Medicine* 159:2349–2356.

Bolles, Richard Nelson, and Mark Emery Bolles. 2005. *What Color Is Your Parachute? 2006: A Practical Manual for Job-Hunters and Career-Changers.* Berkeley: Ten Speed Press.

Branden, Nathaniel. 1985. *Honoring the Self: Self-Esteem and Personal Transformation.* New York: Bantam.

————.1995. *The Six Pillars of Self-Esteem.* New York: Bantam.

————. 1997. *Taking Responsibility.* New York: Fireside.

————. 1998. *How to Raise Your Self-Esteem: The Proven Action-Oriented Approach to Greater Self-Respect and Self-Confidence.* New York: Bantam.

————. 1999. *The Art of Living Consciously: The Power of Awareness to Transform Everyday Life.* New York: Fireside.

Bronson, Po. 2002. *What Should I Do with My Life?* New York: Random House.

Brown, Jane D. 2005. Emerging adults in a media-saturated world. In *Emerging Adults in America: Coming of Age in the Twenty-first Century.* Edited by Jeffrey Arnett and Jennifer Lynn Tanner. Washington, DC: American Psychological Association.

Burns, David D. 1999. *Feeling Good: The New Mood Therapy.* New York: Avon.

Carnevale, Anthony P., Leila Gainer, and Ann Meltzer. 1990. *Workplace Basics: The Essential Skills Employers Want.* San Francisco: Jossey-Bass.

Coelho, Paulo. 1995. *The Alchemist: A Fable About Following Your Dream.* San Francisco: HarperSanFrancisco.

Collins, W. Andrew, and Manfred van Dulmen. 2005. Friendships and romance in emerging adulthood: Assessing distinctiveness in close relationships. In *Emerging Adults in America: Coming of Age in the Twenty-first Century.* Edited by Jeffrey Arnett and Jennifer Lynn Tanner. Washington, DC: American Psychological Association.

Csikszentmihalyi, Mihaly. 1990. *Flow: The Psychology of Optimal Experience.* New York: Perennial.

―――. 1998. *Finding Flow: The Psychology of Engagement with Everyday Life.* New York: Basic Books.

Damasio, Antonio. 1994. *Descartes' Error: Emotion, Reason, and the Human Brain.* New York: Grosset/Putnam.

Dimeo, F. M. Bauer, I. Varahram, G. Proest, and U. Halter. 2001. Benefits from aerobic exercise in patients with major depression: A pilot study. *British Journal of Sports Medicine* 35:114–117.

Earley, P. Christopher, and Soon Ang. 2003. *Cultural Intelligence: Individual Interactions Across Cultures.* Palo Alto, CA: Stanford University Press.

Erickson, Erik. 1994. *Identity: Youth and Crisis.* New York: W. W. Norton & Company.

Fox, Jeffrey J. 2001. *Don't Send a Resume: And Other Contrarian Rules to Help Land a Great Job.* New York: Hyperion.

Frankl, Viktor E. 1997. *Man's Search for Meaning.* New York: Pocket.

Friedman, Howard, and Ronald Riggio. 1981. Effect of individual differences in nonverbal expressiveness on transmission of emotion. *Journal of Nonverbal Behavior* 6(2):96–104.

Friedman, Thomas. 2005a. It's a flat world, after all. *New York Times,* April 3.

―――. 2005b. *The World Is Flat: A Brief History of the Twenty-first Century.* New York: Farrar, Straus and Giroux.

Gates, Bill. 2005. Talk given at the National Education Summit on High School, National Governors Association. February 26.

Gebhard, Nathan, Mike Marriner, and Joanne Gordon. 2003. *Roadtrip Nation: A Guide to Discovering Your Path in Life.* New York: Ballantine Books.

Goleman, Daniel. 1995. *Emotional Intelligence: Why It Can Matter More Than IQ.* New York: Bantam.

———. 1998. *Working with Emotional Intelligence.* New York: Bantam.

Griest, J., M. Klein, R. Eischens, J. Faris, A. Gurman, and W. Morgan. 1979. Running as a treatment for depression. *Comprehensive Psychiatry* 20:41–54.

Hatfield, Elaine, John T. Cacioppo, Richard L. Rapson, Keith Oatley, and Antony Manstead. 1993. *Emotional Contagion.* New York: Cambridge University Press.

Ibarra, Herminia. 2004. *Working Identity: Unconventional Strategies for Reinventing Your Career.* Boston: Harvard Business School Press.

Johnson, Steve, and Matt Murray. 1992. Valedictorians stay level-headed about being No. 1. *Chicago Tribune,* May 29, 1.

Marriner, Mike, Brian McAllister, and Nathan Gebhard. 2005. *Finding the Open Road: A Guide to Self-Construction Rather Than Mass Production.* Berkeley, CA: Ten Speed Press.

McKay, Matthew, and Patrick Fanning. 2000. *Self-Esteem: A Proven Program of Cognitive Techniques for Assessing, Improving, and Maintaining Your Self-Esteem.* Oakland, CA.: New Harbinger Publications.

McKay, Matthew, and Catharine Sutker. 2005. *The Self-Esteem Guided Journal.* Oakland, CA: New Harbinger Publications.

Pennebaker, James W. 1997. *Opening Up: The Healing Power of Expressing Emotions.* New York: Guilford Press.

Pink, Daniel. 2005. *A Whole New Mind: Moving from the Information Age to the Conceptual Age.* New York: Riverhead.

Salazar, Marcos. 2001. *Feeling Good for Life: The Clinically Proven Exercise and Diet Program That will Help Burn Fat, Build Muscle, Boost Your Mood, and Conquer Depression.* Lincoln, NE: Writer's Club Press.

Schwartz, Barry. 2003. *The Paradox of Choice: Why More Is Less.* New York: Ecco.

Seligman, Martin. 1993. *Learned Helplessness: A Theory for the Age of Personal Control.* New York: Oxford University Press.

———. 1998. *Learned Optimism: How to Change Your Mind and Your Life.* New York: Free Press.

———. 2004. *Authentic Happiness: Using the New Positive Psychology to Realize Your Potential for Lasting Fulfillment.* New York: Free Press.

Spera, Stephanie, Eric Buhrfeind, and James Pennebaker. 1994. Expressive writing and coping with job loss. *Academy of Management Journal* 37:722–733.

U.S. Census Bureau. 2000. Current Population Reports. Estimated Age at First Marriage.

Watters, Ethan. 2003. *Urban Tribes: A Generation Redefines Friendship, Family, and Commitment.* New York: Bloomsbury USA.

Marcos Salazar is a researcher for the American Psychological Association, where he studies trends in the workforce and education system within psychology. He is a certified leadership coach by The George Washington University and specializes in life coaching for twentysomethings. He is also co-owner of Slaphappy Ventures, LLC, which operates **www.DistrictTees com** and **www.Slaphappy Tees.com.**